Praise for Jim Crum

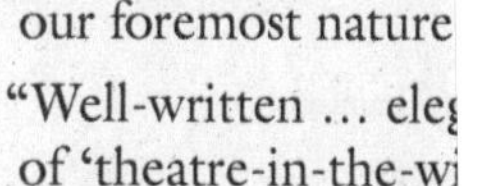

“Crumley has earned
our foremost nature

“Well-written … eleg
of ‘theatre-in-the-wi

“Crumley conveys th
at its wildest … with honesty and passion and, yes, poetry.” —*Scottish Review of Books*

“Close observations … from the February song of a mistle thrush to May’s drowsy warmth.” —*New Statesman*

“Scotland’s pre-eminent nature writer.” —*Guardian*

“Enthralling and often strident.” —*Observer*

“Virtuoso writing.” —Paul Evans, *BBC Countryfile*

“Crumley’s distinctive voice carries you with him on his dawn forays.” —John Lister-Kaye, *Herald*

“The best nature writer working in Britain today.” —David Craig, *Los Angeles Times*

“Compulsively descriptive and infectious in its enthusiasm.” —*Scotland on Sunday*

“Glowing and compelling.” —*Countryman*

“Nature writing is like trying to catch birds with cobwebs. Crumley’s just has a higher tensile strength than most.” —Brian Morton, *Herald*

“Combines an extraordinary depth of detailed, recorded knowledge with vivid warm writing … enchanting.” —Sara Maitland, *BBC Countryfile*

“Powerful descriptions … a cornucopia of autumnal delight.” —Polly Pullar, *The Scots Magazine*

The Eagle’s Way was shortlisted for a Saltire Society Literary Award in 2014.

Selected list of books by Jim Crumley

NATURE WRITING

Seasons of Stom and Wonder
Lakeland Wild
Nature's Architect
The Eagle's Way
The Great Wood
The Last Wolf
The Winter Whale
Brother Nature
Something Out There
A High and Lonely Place
The Company of Swans
Gulfs of Blue Air
The Heart of the Cairngorms
The Heart of Mull
The Heart of Skye
Among Mountains
Among Islands
Badgers on the Highland Edge
Waters of the Wild Swan
The Pentland Hills
Shetland – Land of the Ocean
Glencoe – Monarch of Glens
West Highland Landscape
St Kilda

ENCOUNTERS IN THE WILD SERIES:
Fox, Barn Owl, Swan, Hare,
Badger, Skylark, Kingfisher, Otter

IN THE MOMENT

Watching Wildlife

Jim Crumley

Saraband

Published by Saraband
3 Clairmont Gardens
Glasgow, G3 7LW
www.saraband.net

ISBN: 9781913393847
eISBN: 9781915089946

Note: Units of measure are given either in Imperial or Metric, depending on those best suited in each instance.

Printed and bound in Great Britain by Clays Ltd, Elcograf S.p.A.

1 2 3 4 5 6 7 8 9 10

"My one salvation, a gift I can't reason through, has been the unceasing kindness of animals."

—Barry Lopez, *Field Notes*, 1994

Contents

The Bit at the Start

It recurs again and again, it has done throughout my nature writing life, and I cannot imagine it will stop until I do: it is the question, often couched in hints of scepticism, "How come you see so much wildlife?" The answer is a prosaic one. It's because I spend such a disproportionate amount of time looking for it. And, perhaps it is more accurate to say, waiting for it to turn up.

At its most disproportionate, I studied a single mute swan territory for roughly thirty years. I did other things as well during those thirty years, but the study itself occupied literally thousands of hours. The swans' lifestyle broke all the rules and contradicted all the field guide generalities. Their landscape was a reed bed in a bay at the north end of a long, narrow, curving loch tucked under the first mountain of Highland Scotland if you travel northwest out of Stirling. That landscape has been my workaday habit for decades. They shared that landscape with two kinds of eagles, two kinds of deer, otters, pine martens, badgers, beavers, foxes, fluctuating hordes of wildfowl, Atlantic salmon, pike and a heronry. To my certain knowledge, the principals of the study – the original cob and pen – lived for at least thirty and twenty-five years respectively.

Quite apart from the raw beauty of their chosen landscape and the constant walk-on parts for their diverse wildlife neighbours, the swans were required to overcome a formidable natural adversity almost every year: their nesting season was routinely tormented by floods that washed out nest after nest and clutch of eggs after clutch of eggs. In one spring and early summer that was painful to watch and is still painful to recount, they lost four nests and four clutches of eggs and finally hatched a single cygnet on a fifth nest in July. Mute swan nests are vast. The labour involved was as heroic as it was bloody-minded.

Even so, I hear you say, you watched for *thirty* years? Yes, and it does sound disproportionate. And yet, and yet: that swan-watching project led directly to a series of radio programmes on BBC Radio 4, two books – *Waters of the Wild Swan* and *The Company of Swans*, a BBC television programme in the "Wildlife on One" series, and a long-standing working relationship with the BBC Natural History Unit radio producer Grant Sonnex which would take me to Alaska for three weeks, and to Iceland and Norway for a week at a time, all of which helped fuel a passion for wolves, grizzly bears, humpback whales … as well as various tribes of wild swans.

There is also this. The wildlife encounters I write about are the fruits of the memorable days, and these are outnumbered (I would guess) ten to one by those days when very little or nothing at all happens, and no one wants to read about those, any more than I want to write about them. But even these days have a value for the nature writer because you learn more about the landscapes where you work, about patterns and rhythms in the wild year; and if you go often enough for long enough, you bear witness to incremental change in those rhythms and patterns and you try to reason why.

The title of this series of books, "In the Moment", is a perfect summary of what follows. Each chapter centres on a species with which I am reasonably familiar, and the particular encounters have been chosen because, to my mind, they constitute defining moments in the inexact art of watching wildlife, in my writing life. And being in the moment is the ultimate reward. It is not television, and it is not reading about someone else's moment in someone else's book; it is participating, being part of nature yourself. The inevitable result is that your respect for nature deepens, as does your own awareness of your own place within nature.

Never in human history has it been more important that we develop a deeper respect for our planet. So, go and find yourself some moments in nature's company.

Golden Eagle

Golden eagles are not hard to see, but nor are they easy to watch for long. Most mountaineers in the Highlands and Islands have golden eagle stories to tell but they are stories of glimpses a few seconds long or, exceptionally, a few minutes. There are two good reasons why. One is that the mountaineer's priority is the mountain, and a glimpse of an eagle is but an embellishment on the mountain day. His next mountain day will almost always be on a different mountain. The other reason is that, historically, the golden eagle has good reason to avoid people and is hypersensitive to disturbance by them. For example, you would never catch a golden eagle following a boat full of passengers with telephoto lenses the size of baseball bats, nor diving down to snatch from the surface a fish thrown from such a boat. A sea eagle will do this. A sea eagle does not disdain humanity. A sea eagle is a generalist in its feeding habits. A golden eagle is a specialist.

I am something of a reformed mountaineer. I evolved into a nature writer. The transition required me to stop changing mountains every time I went out. It also required me to change the way I climbed that particular mountain on which golden eagles are a reliable presence, so that the greater understanding of the way eagles use their territory became the summit I sought, the same summit every time, the pursuit of intimacy. Over years, the eagles and I fashioned a kind of spasmodic co-existence until eventually I became a sometimes mobile, sometimes static component of their landscape. Such a relationship is of no value to a mountaineer. To a nature writer, it is gold dust.

The glen that accommodates the golden eagle eyrie I have in mind ends abruptly in a wide headwall, lightly wooded mostly with birch, craggy, bouldery and bisected by a white-knuckled burn whose procession of waterfalls echoes far and wide. This is how it works when I climb into the eagles' workaday landscape.

Late on a June evening, the glen softened by shadow after a long day of sunshine and trekking across the eagles' territory, I had paused by a certain rock with long views to the distant eyrie. I was rewinding the day's events in my mind when a ring ouzel started singing. The song is full of jazzy rhythms and a tendency to belt out one haunting note again and again between phrases, like Sweets Edison used to do (Sweets is remembered for his muted, jazzy trumpet fill-ins on the best albums of Frank Sinatra, Ella Fitzgerald, Tony Bennett, as well as a timelessly bluesy soloist in the company of such as Oscar Peterson, Lester Young...). On and on, the song flowed with the fluency of mountain burns, and then I thought I might sit where I could see the singer. So I crawled away from the rock, my chin in the heather, one slow yard at a time. The ouzel was twenty yards away in a small birch tree by the burn, his back to the rock. I crawled into the lee of a smaller rock, put my back to it and simply sat there. If the bird turned round, I would be in full view, but I was dressed in something like the shades of the rock and the land, and I was silent and still, and these things always help.

Then the fox showed up.

It trotted along its accustomed path, one fox wide, but as it neared the ouzel's tree it slowed its pace then stopped. Then it sat. Then it put its head on one side. And if you were to ask me what I think it was doing, and if I thought you were not the kind of person easily given to ridicule, I would tell you that I think it was listening to the music, as I was myself. But now I was listening to the music while also watching the fox listening to the music while both of us were also watching the musician, who seemed to be oblivious to both of us. For three, perhaps four minutes, this situation prevailed.

It all ended abruptly. The ouzel simply stopped singing of its own accord and flew off into the deepening shadows of the burn. The fox scratched its nose with a forepaw, stood up and wandered off.

I don't really know what the fox was doing, only that it seemed to be fascinated by the bird, and the only fascinating thing the bird was doing was singing. Nothing in the fox's behaviour suggested it was stalking the bird. And, as far as I could see, it was doing exactly what I was doing, nothing more, nothing less.

I know this, though. If you spend a lot of time in one place with one overriding purpose centred on one particular species (in this case, the eagle glen and its eagles), you also learn about some of the eagles' neighbours and fellow-travellers too, just because you are out there and for long periods you are quite still and the neighbours and the fellow-travellers go about their workaday business, and you see at firsthand how they get on with each other and how they treat you like a bit of their landscape. There are days in this glen when you see no eagles at all, and a handful of days when they are rarely out of sight, but there are no days when you see nothing at all.

So each time I climb the burn at the right season of the year, en route to the watershed, I stop some distance short of the rock by the stunted birch and listen and watch and wait, just in case. And because I have gone often enough for long enough, I now know that the ring ouzel is an unpredictable presence in the glen, that there are years when the bird is a regrettable absence, but also that sooner or later it returns, or its offspring do. And this is what I mean by learning to climb the mountain differently, and this is what I mean when I say that my eagle watching has been folded into the raw stuff of my nature-writing life.

*

The pale female eagle found me at the watcher's rock, crossing the glen 200 feet above me, but looking down, noticing. My sense of being watched was profound. There was no ring ouzel singing, and if the dog fox was out I did not see him. What I do know is that he no longer has any cubs this year, for the eagles took all three, one by one, and sometimes that too is part of the story of how the creatures of the glen get on with their neighbours. The pale female circled, a wide and leisurely circle with the big rock at its centre, and maybe she did that every time and maybe she only did it if I was there, but how would I know?

I paused halfway on my climb up the headwall. The only long view was behind me, back down the entire length of the upper glen, which has something of the feel of a steep-sided alpine meadow; beyond, the descent steepens through forest and the burn becomes a turbulent river hell-bent on the loch, two miles distant and a thousand feet lower.

Then the slope of the headwall relented suddenly, and the flanks of the glen fell away behind, and ahead the watershed opened and sprawled. The solitary cairn beckoned like a wild rose to a bee; the transformation in the nature of the land was instant and utter. Here, on the right kind of day, there unfurls such a breadth of heartland mountains cramming the horizon from east to west and folding away improbable distances northwards, that you are aware of the catch in your breath and the uncertainty of your eyes as they struggle to take it all in. Sometimes, on the blue moon days, I have seen an eagle or a pair of eagles rise against the mountain horizon and on up into skies without limits, which is when and where you learn things about the eagles that you never see and never learn from a hide. They don't inhabit the world as constrained by the window of a hide or the lenses of camera or binoculars. They inhabit this world, this their three-dimensional territory, and they embody a mastery of airspace as virtuosic as any creature that ever drew breath. Nothing is beyond them here: 100 miles per hour in a shallow glide with wings half folded and unbeating; a 3,000-foot freefall that ends fifty feet above the ground and segues into a 1,000-foot power-climb, then another freefall and the softest of soft landings on the frond of a rowan sapling. I have even seen the pale eagle rise on a thermal alongside a cliff and, with her feet down and her wings wide, urge the wind to drift her purposefully – playfully – backwards through the air. Her mate also knows that trick, and I wonder if one has taught it to the other.

The watershed itself sends its infant burns south and north, and these, though they rise within yards of each other, are destined one for the Forth and one for the Tay, and if their paths ever cross at all it must be somewhere around the Bell Rock lighthouse, fifteen miles out into the North Sea from Arbroath on the Angus coast. The abrupt headwall of the eagle glen may be behind and below and in the south, but the watershed itself is a gentler land, wide and turned up at the edges towards east and west, and dipping gently to the north, where long, easy slopes slide away to one of the great east–west crossings of all Scotland.

So this watershed, this plain in the sky, is the tract of land that sustains the very heartbeat of the eagles' territory. I lived down there to the north at the foot of these long slopes for five years, and I learned a lot about golden eagle territories (and a bit about myself) during that time. It seemed to me that their territories had more to do with wind direction than physical boundaries. That there were, for example, negotiable overlapping areas between this territory and the nearest one to the east, because the birds themselves seem to prefer to hunt into the wind, for it affords them more flight control; so if there was a west wind blowing, the hunting birds from both pairs would be out in the western reaches of their territories, and a tailwind would ease their burdened journeys back to their eyries. At that time, both pairs prospered from a superabundance of rabbits on the lower slopes above the cottage where I lived, and on several occasions I saw birds from both eyries working the same hillside, which I assumed to be part of the negotiable terrain. But during the nesting season this watershed is the exclusive preserve of the pale female and her mate, and another eagle straying this close to the eyrie meets with aggressive intolerance. In late summer and autumn the boundaries relax. I have – once and only once – seen the four adults and the two single chicks they fledged lazily afloat on a warm late-September afternoon, the terrier-yaps of the young birds falling a thousand feet down the sky. All six birds were high above these north-facing slopes where that brief era of rabbit plenty had perhaps afforded some kind of common ground and mutual tolerance on the brief days of the wild year when the living was easy. The golden eagle's nesting season is a long one. By the end of December the courting overtures that reinforce territorial boundaries will have begun again, and so will old hostilities.

*

I had climbed to the cairn after my morning by the big rock on the floor of the upper glen and its encounter with the pale eagle; I had marvelled at the far-flung, wide-slung sprawl of mountains beyond; I had blessed my good luck and my gratitude at being in such a place on such a day; and I had settled by the cairn, unpacked my lunch and my notebook, and unslung my binoculars from my neck and put them down on a flat stone where my right hand would find them. This is my idea of a working lunch. I kept looking east across the watershed and south-east across the ridge where the eagle disappeared. Occasionally I scanned the whole sky through 360 degrees, then all the ridges down both sides of the glen, and then (and this is the hard part) the spaces *between* mountain walls.

I don't know how many years it would have taken me before I tumbled to the fact that the place the eagle is most likely to be at any one time is somewhere in the space between mountain walls, but it was the nature writer and golden eagle obsessive Mike Tomkies who told me: "You *must* learn to scan the middle distance." It sounds obvious now, but when we met he had already logged many hundreds of hours of watching golden eagles from hides he built himself from the raw stuff of the mountainside, and this piece of advice was one of the many fruits of his labours. The trouble with the middle distance is that it has no focal points, other than the birds that fly through it. Mike became a friend and was generous with his time and his knowledge. When he died in 2016, nature surely mourned the loss of an ambassador to its cause. He had served eagles particularly well.

By late afternoon I was thinking of calling it a day. It was still an hour and a half back down to the car, although, as I have ruefully pointed out to myself many, many times, about three minutes for a golden eagle that chooses to put its mind to the task. Vigils like this work up to a pitch, a plateau of intensity when my absorption in my surroundings is so complete that every sense is vitally alert and almost beyond the possibility of distraction. But eventually the mind drifts and the eyes tire. It's usually a good indicator that I have stopped being useful to myself, or in other words, time to go home. One last check with the glasses through one last lingering scrutiny of the slopes, the sky, finally the middle distance, and there was that something, that sudden "?"

What did I just see?

Where?

I retraced that last sweep of the glasses, up and down, side to side, all the way across those northern slopes. Nothing. Again. Then again.

Then ... far, far down the mountainside I found the one thing that changed everything: a rock that didn't look quite right. There had been dark movement that stopped and settled as the glasses swept past the rock, then the question, then the re-examination of the landscape, then the rock, the rock that hosted what was surely a sea eagle. If it had been a golden eagle, I would have stayed on the watershed, banking on the probability that its next move would have been back towards the heart of the territory. But a sea eagle is more likely to be wandering the big east–west valley with its rivers and lochs. So I held a short discussion with myself about how I might close the distance to the rock without disturbing the eagle. I opted for the course of a burn that slithered through head-high heathery banks. But if I was to be unobserved as I travelled, I would not be able to see the rock, or the eagle if it moved. The going was messy, awkward, and several misjudgements of my left foot gave me a trouser leg wet up to the knee. A cautious approach to a dip in the top of the bank might let me look at the rock, but now it was hidden by a small rise in the hillside, so perhaps if I crawled the fifty yards to the top, all would be clear. Halfway there, it occurred to me, a little belatedly, that if I could see this sea eagle from the watershed, either of the resident golden eagles could have seen it from several times that distance, and it was unlikely, to put it mildly, that they would leave it in peace.

I had still about ten yards to go to the crest of the rise when the huge raised primary feathers of an eagle appeared against the sky dead ahead, followed at once by the rest of the bird – the sea eagle – travelling uphill at speed and no more than ten feet off the ground. I froze, on all fours, my left hand and left knee ahead of my right. It was that bizarre and quite possibly unfathomable creature the sea eagle saw as it crossed the rise so close to me that its wingbeats sounded like rhythmic gusts of a gale – *whoof, whoof, whoof* – that made the hill grasses tremble. The eagle banked to pass me on my left. I remember staring into eagle eyes with the sun full on them, one either side of the biggest, yellowest slap of hooked beak in all these skies, the bunched fists of stowed talons, the simply colossal wings. Then clear sky.

Ah, but then there was the shadow.

It toppled over the edge of the rise and came straight at me. Considering how often I have symbolised the passage of the shadow of an eagle across a mountainside, both in my mind and in print, and the fear and sense of subservience that passage must inflict on the mountain's lesser creatures, I eyed this approaching shadow with a kind of dread. A collision was unavoidable. There was a split second – surely imagined – of profound chill, then the sun was on my back again and the thing was done.

Or not.

The crest was not done with me yet. It now unleashed a golden eagle, the pale female of the morning's encounter in pursuit of the sea eagle, but at the sight of me (and being a flier of an altogether more exalted class than its quarry), it soared on unbeating wings, gained fifty feet of altitude in a moment and drifted away east, still climbing.

All this, from beginning to end, had consumed perhaps twenty seconds.

I turned to look for the two eagles, the one last seen heading south-west, the other east. At first there was nothing at all, but then the sea eagle drifted by, having climbed a couple of hundred feet and turned away, heading north-west. It crossed a hill shoulder and was gone. The golden eagle was circling, not a quarter of a mile away and slightly uphill from me. Then she levelled out and drove straight towards me, circled once a hundred feet above my head, then flew west, and I wondered if in her own mind she had just etched a line of demarcation for the sea eagle's benefit – this far, and no further.

I waved to her. Why? Because it's a thing I do. I ritualise my presence on her mountainsides, and she is accustomed to it.

*

Sometimes the eagle watcher in me prefers Scotland's island west to its Highland midst. I have a taste for the off-piste in islands. For example, you don't see many postcards of the high moors above Bracadale or the River Snizort in Skye's tourist information centres. The Snizort was never the most expressive of rivers, and when I found it one September-into-October morning, it was as reluctant to stir itself as a hedgehog in January, sluggish as a duck in mud. The day was warm and windless, rain fell soft and thick and ruthless. The river was swollen with its own too-muchness, and its peaty banks trembled at its own peat-stained power. There was something morose in the air. You make what you can of such days if you are a nature writer.

My relationship with water is complex. I read in a book called *Water Always Wins: Thriving in an Age of Drought and Deluge*, by Erica Gies (Head of Zeus, 2022), that many North American indigenous traditions don't consider water to be a "what" but a "who", not a commodity – and far less a threat – but a living entity, even kin. I have sympathy for the idea, not least because such an attitude must surely lead to a much more considerate and protective relationship with how they use water.

It was easy on that Skye morning, the dawning of the third such consecutive day, to invest the Snizort with animistic character traits, for it was exploring new territory from the day before and its vocal range was more diverse and expressive. In an age of drought and deluge, water – the lack of it or the superabundance of it – will have a lot to say to us over the next few decades. One of the smartest things we can do as we contemplate the climate monster we have spawned is to liberate water, to find ways of abandoning our age-old determination to control it, and let it flow where it wants. That single course of action, liberally applied, would be seen by historians of the future as the moment when we decided to enter into a new partnership with nature as just one more of nature's creatures rather than as a tribe that likes to think we can rule the world. We can't. We never could. We never will.

Such was the train of thought that spilled into the sodden world of the River Snizort, which was contemplating a new life beyond its banks, as if the idea was one that it had held in check for decades, centuries perhaps, but now had given voice to again in response to its sudden liberation. I saw the river in a new light that morning, considered it as an ambassador for our relationship with all the world's rivers, thought it might approve, and I moved easily from there to the idea that I might match my mood that day to nature's mood, and move more contentedly through the landscape, keeping the river's company. My long experience of Skye, more than fifty years of it, long since concluded that September-into-October was the best of it, that it was more at ease with itself then than at any other time of the year, that it was a kind of slack water of the seasons, a brimful tidal pool. The morning was a riot of greys, visibility cordoned off by a circle of wet cloud and mist (and where one ended and the other began was a thing of guesswork that was barely worth the effort), but if you would match your mood with nature's, you can settle agreeably enough into even that monochromatic ethos.

Then, just when I began to think that I was the only one of nature's creatures on the prowl that morning, five mallards leapt from the newly redefined river, I think perhaps more from astonishment than alarm. I followed their flight for as long as my eyes could hold on to it in the murk, for apart from myself and the river they were the morning's only moving fragments. They circled back overhead, quacking like every cartoon duck you ever heard and, apart from the river talking to itself, theirs was the only conversation I would hear for hours. I unsheathed binoculars from the inside of my jacket and followed them for all of fifty yards before I lost them to the rain and the mist and the cloud and the land-devouring grey.

Given that I had gone to the trouble of bringing the glasses to bear, I cast around with them anyway, suppressing a long-held belief acquired from my mountaineering years that once you have seen the inside of one cloud you have seen the inside of them all. I swung them through a slow sweep of the horizonless world. Somewhere between north and south-south-east (who knows in *this*?) there was a discernibly mobile fragment of low hillside. I overshot it of course, for I had expected nothing at all, but habit and experience stopped the binoculars in mid-sweep and inched them slowly back in the opposite direction. What I found was a moor-quartering golden eagle. You *must* learn to scan the middle distance. Remember? It is a tricky art at the best of times but on a day such as that one, there was only middle distance, and anything that moved was self-evident simply because it was the only thing that did.

She worked the land. I decided she was female on the basis of her great size, but that could well have been a trick of the light, or rather the absence of light, the absence of anything to provide scale, but if you watch eagles often enough over enough years and in many different circumstances, you provide your own sense of scale. She was crossing and re-crossing the same hillside as diligently methodical as a horse-drawn plough. In that time she was never higher than six feet above the moor. Often less. But she did not touch it once. Yet the wings barely moved. Restraint. Fluency. Unflinching purpose. A masterclass in the art of flight in the slow lane.

Once, she dipped a wing and dropped to within inches of the ground, so low and slow now that she must surely land. But she checked even that descent, levelled out, laid open her wings and let whatever it is that lifts an eagle a foot in the air lift her. It was eagle watching at its most addictively hypnotic.

She exhausted the slope's possibilities. She rose through the curtains of mist and rain in three wing-beats, the strides of giants. She was first a blur and then an absence.

It is not hard to see eagles on Skye once you know where to look and what you are looking for and you have learned to filter out the buzzards. Nesting ledges abound and there are good open tracts for hunting. Even so, the chances of a solitary human hell-bent on making the most of such a day and a solitary hunting eagle coinciding for ten unbroken minutes on the same quarter-of-a-square-mile are not high.

The change began in the north. The rain eased, then stopped. Mist receded, vanished. I felt wind on my face, light and cool. I peeled off the waterproof layer. It was like stepping from a chrysalis and discovering flight. An hour later, 1,200 feet up and atop a crag, I watched the sun tunnel through, saw quicksilver Skye turn the landscape's tears to sequins. I wondered where the eagle was. Someone told me not long ago that I was lucky to see so much. And I remembered the golfer Gary Player's response to a journalist who suggested an extravagantly holed bunker shot was "a bit lucky".

"The thing is," said Player, "the more I practise them, the luckier I get."

*

So, for all the endless hours of being out there, the honing and refining of carefully devised routines, the slow accumulation of the strands of your idea of what a golden eagle is and how it works and why it does certain things that don't appear to make sense to non-eagles, never ever discount the one great indefinable essential which no naturalist and no nature writer can do without: luck. There is nothing more gratifying in the limitless scope of watching wildlife the world over than turning up in the right time at the right place. And the more you practise …

The Sleat peninsula is southmost Skye, and it, too, satisfies my desire for the off-piste. On an afternoon of late winter after a long, tiring day, I got back to the car, chose a piece of music and set off on the short drive back across the peninsula to Isleornsay, where I was staying for a few days. I ambled round Tarskavaig Bay and turned into that tight and twisty gorge that clambers up among fractured moors giddy with hill burns, freckled with lochans. The music was the guitarist John Williams playing

Rodrigo's "Fantasía Para Un Gentilhombre", the first movement of which ended as I emerged from the trees of the gorge into a moment of divine timelessness. At the precise moment of that brief silence between the end of the first movement and the beginning of the second, a golden eagle slid low over the crest of a hill called Sithean Mor, edging more or less east below the skyline. It dipped and slowed to that familiar hunting gait, that purposeful dawdle just a yard above the surface of the hillside and a breath above stalling speed. At that moment, the music resumed.

At the first notes of the adagio, a slow, stalking, low-register guitar theme, I had an extraordinary sense of orchestrating the eagle flight, so powerfully did bird and guitar dovetail. Had it been a film, this was a score by John Barry, say, and the daring director could have been Sydney Pollack. Think *Out of Africa*. The eagle began to travel the hillside at the same slow-motion pace, a single wingbeat sustaining the headway at intervals of about fifty yards, parallel to the road and perhaps fifty feet above it while the music spun out its own inexorable thread of golden brown. I had stopped the car by now, lowered the window, craning to follow the flight. I felt the first splashes of a fast and light ocean shower spatter my face, sharp and soft at the same time, a kindly sting.

The bird flew on, still following the line of the hill and hill road, and I had the bizarre idea that I could stalk the eagle in the car. I set off on the most enthralling and unlikely mile I have ever driven, although the speed never rose above fifteen miles per hour and I diced several times with the rocky and ditched roadside with my eyes firmly on the eagle. At every dip or bend or brief blindness in the road, I was sure I would emerge beyond it to find the eagle had disappeared, but each time I found the bird again at once, still holding its course and its altitude. I fell in behind it again on the empty road while the music mimicked the bird's fluidity, or the other way round, a flawless unison that went beyond just listening, just watching.

The music changed the mood abruptly, for the composer interrupts the adagio's flow with first a fanfare then a dance, and at that point I devised a new ploy. I would overtake the eagle. I would park beyond the summit of the road and wait for it there, perhaps photograph it as it flew past. So while the fanfares and two-steps filled the car and drifted out into the uncaring airspace of south Skye, I negotiated a bend or two, crossed the summit, parked, grabbed the camera and waited for the eagle to reappear while the music eschewed the dance and slipped back into the reprise of the adagio's theme.

The eagle completed the sequence perfectly on cue, and the unanimity of music and flight resumed. Then as it drew level with the car and perhaps fifty yards away, it snapped the spell with a powerful, swerving climb up the hillside, lifted above the skyline in a handful of seconds, burnished gold in the sunset light. Three more wingbeats and it vanished beyond the hill crest. I said one word, out loud:

"Cut."

Moments like these, when you are handed a glimpse of something within nature that is beyond what you have seen and what you have known before ... these moments occur at long intervals and only because you go out again and again and again and try to add to your store of understanding, and these are the golden moments.

Once in a while I replay the moment in my mind, stimulated by the drop of an eagle wing, or perhaps when the right frame of mind coincides with the recording of John Williams playing the "Fantasía", or perhaps when (because I still go to Sleat from time to time) I point my car up through that tight and twisty gorge that clambers up among the fractured moors giddy with hill burns, freckled with lochans.

Otter

One of the things I love best about islands is beachcombing. For otters.

On the west coast of Mull there is a shore so liberally awash with a species of broad-leaved wrack that it turns every other wave and ripple into otter false alarms, the more so if you know that otters live here, that you will usually have the shore to yourself, that with an onshore wind and a falling tide the prospects of seeing otters are good. All you have to do is stick around. A flat rock strewn with the debris of an otter meal of fresh crab is worth watching. Experience tells you that, and so does common sense. Make yourself comfortable (a relative state of affairs on a rocky, seaweedy Hebridean shore) – if there is still no trace of the diner two hours later, that just confirms the self-evident truth that beachcombing, whether for otters or anything else, is an inexact science.

In time, in time, out there amid the suck and blow of slow, shallow waves beneath the whispering seaweed, there was a furrow that was surely too straight to be the work of a conspiracy of wrack and rock. But it was not an otter. It was two otters, swimming deliberately nose-to-tail and straight as a washed-up mast from Nova Scotia. I was sitting on a low ledge of a small cliff, ready to move closer to the water's edge whenever the otters dived, but they did not dive. Instead, the leading otter turned at right angles and straight towards me. The second otter followed suit. The leading otter kept uttering that familiar, hoarse, interrogative-sounding *Haah*? It asks three questions: who are you, what are you and what are you doing here?

Both otters stood on hind legs in the shallows and barked the same question in unison. When I failed to respond with either sound or gesture, one of the otters either lost interest or lost its nerve, executed a neat back flip, rolled away into deep water and vanished. But the first otter still stood its ground, still stood erect, and demanded *Haah*? every few seconds. I have met this phenomenon before and, by copying their sound, I have – occasionally – participated in a conversation lasting several minutes without understanding a single syllable. Mostly, nature ignores this kind of mimicry, but – again only occasionally – it can lure the creature closer. And for the weasel tribe to which otters belong, curiosity is part of their workaday lives. Then the second otter reappeared.

It was a beautifully built, thick-set dog otter and at once he began swimming and stomping all around the bitch, trying (it seemed to me) to deflect her obsessive interest in the non-otter on the shore. He barrel-rolled in the water, which impressed me more than it did her, for she turned on him in a lithe and leathery swirl, snapped her jaws close to his muzzle, turned in less than her own length and was once again standing – and out of the water now – and challenging me again: *Haah*?

The dog otter repeatedly lured her into the water where she toyed with him, snapped at him, then returned to stand and stare at me. Once, she uncoiled back into the water and dived through whirlpools of her own making. In the flowing of the two otters, the surge and retreat of water and the restless heave of the seaweed, nature contrived a mobile jigsaw puzzle in which all of the pieces constantly moved but none of them was ever out of place, the puzzle never incomplete.

This kind of interaction with nature has given me some of the most precious moments of my life. But I love it best when it happens entirely on nature's terms. I have never been much of a fan of luring animals into a situation where they effectively become performers for a human audience. There are naturalists, writers, photographers, tourism operators who can achieve spectacular results with a lure of some kind. I don't decry it, but it's not for me. When Mike Tomkies lived in the cottage he called Wildernesse on Loch Shiel, he tamed a pine marten he called Micky to such an extent that it would come in the window onto his desk and take a piece of jammy bread from his mouth. I saw it happen. There is no denying that when he wrote about it, it won many new friends for pine martens. But it made me wince.

The otter bitch was back, and on her hind legs again. The otter's capacity for play is biological fact. This one had apparently decided to rope me in. It began with my mimicry of her voice. Every time she returned to the shore she stood and said: *Haah?* If I failed to respond at once, she would repeat it and go on repeating it until I did respond, at which point she would whirl round and dive into the waves again. Then she added a new twist. She squirmed along a rock ledge just above the sea and vanished where the ledge vanished behind the rock. Her tail was the last of her to vanish. Seconds later her head – just her head – reappeared where her tail had just been, and she barked at me again. I responded. She reversed out of sight. Then she inched forward again and peered round the rock.

Haah? she said again.

I sat motionless, soundless, suppressing the urge to laugh and to run and hide myself.

She got bored.

Then she leaped off the rock, and in my mind as I write this is an image of her frozen in mid-air, all four legs splayed wide, her tail straight out, her jaws wide open. And in that attitude she thudded into the water with an enormous splash and the two otters rolled away from the chaos.

The next I saw of them they were a hundred yards away, swimming companionably north. I wonder what otters do when they swim off knowing they have beguiled a human bystander. Perhaps they experience no aftermath at all and they are already preoccupied with what's next in their lives. Perhaps the only aftermath was mine, and that will last a lifetime for this beguiled island wanderer who loves nothing better than to go beachcombing for otters.

Gavin Maxwell wrote in *Ring of Bright Water*:

> *There is a perpetual mystery and excitement in living on the seashore, which is in part a return to childhood and in part because for all of us the sea's edge remains the edge of the unknown; the child sees the bright shells, the vivid weeds and red sea-anemones of the rock pools with wonder and with the child's eye for minutiae; the adult who retains wonder brings to his gaze some partial knowledge which can but increase it, and he brings, too, the eye of association and of symbolism, so that the edge of the ocean he stands at the brink of his own unconscious.*

Sitting at the edge of the ocean, I suddenly wanted to drink to that. As it happened, I had a small hipflask. I tilted it, spared a thought for the memory of the writer, and drank. The slow fires of Talisker were as icing on the cake of my wellbeing, and briefly that ultimate savour of the Isle of Skye imbued the many richnesses of the Isle of Mull. It's a good country I live in.

*

Talisker is five things: that whisky (which has exalted the word throughout the whisky-drinking world), a bay, a beautiful house, a river and a burn that crosses a flat shelf of land in a straight line between house and shore and meets the river there. It is hard to imagine a more perfect place for otters, or for a wandering nature writer. A dipper's arrowhead zips seawards a foot above the burn's golden-brown mile, low enough for its white breast to show in the water as a pale blur.

The musky language of spraints punctuates the bank of the burn. They say an otter has passed. So do five-toed footprints in the mud, for that matter, but if you have an eye practised in reading the runes of the spraints, they can tell you – roughly – how long gone the otter may be: very long gone and the spraint is grey or white, brittle and scentless; just gone and it is wet and soft and dark and musky. That much is comparatively easy. But to an otter nose a spraint tells which otter has passed, alone or in company, and whether or not it has any business being there. Conspicuous flat rocks or grassy projections are favourite places.

As for the otter itself, you can see it here at its most amphibious best. As always, patience, persistence and luck have their own rewards. When I think of it now, I remember the third consecutive early morning walking the burn west, towards the sea. I became aware of the otter (how often that happens in the middle of the view, and I never saw it arrive), and it was fifty yards ahead of me and weaseling along the bank, rippling as it ran, and what with the trees that flank the inland stretch of the burn and the low sunlight, it dappled as it rippled. Its fur was pale and dry and thick, which is the otter as most people don't see it, for it had been sleeping or sunning itself or both and was newly roused, ready for the hunt. Brightness flooded the burn where the trees ended, and there the otter took to the water at once. Just as I convinced myself that that was the last I would see of it (for in my mind's eye it was headed flat-out for the river and the sea beyond), the bubbling wake of the underwater swimmer appeared travelling upstream, towards me. Be still.

When it swam past, it was six feet away, and the shadow it threw onto the bed of the burn was just ahead and slightly to its left. The otter curved towards a tiny slope on the further bank, cruised ashore and hit it running. It was twenty yards away with its back to me when it stopped dead and turned its head and neck. One foot was raised like a pointer, but while it pointed upstream it stared at me. Now the fur was sleek and dark and the otter shape streamlined, barely recognisable as the bank-running animal of a minute before. And then there was that single syllable again, that questioning something somewhere between a grunted bark and a gasp. With a movement as fluid as oil on marble, the otter flowed back into the burn and swam past me again. This time the shadow trailed behind.

For as long as it swam underwater, I could follow as quickly as I liked, ready to crouch and freeze when it surfaced. It was about eighty yards ahead when it emerged on to the bank. I crouched and froze. The otter looked back. He would see my crouch and know exactly what it represented. But that weasel curiosity got the better of it. It stood on its hind legs, the better to see and scent. It makes the animal look like what it is not. All the way from a weasel to a bear, the pose is the same. The glasses revealed an old, grey-muzzled dog otter, wearing lightly the wisdom of its years. It moved from water on to land and back without a break in its stride, without interruption to the fluidity and fluency of movement: it ran like a swimmer and swam like a runner, but when it stood, it stood like a weasel.

I have acquired some idea by now (over decades of otter watching and being otter-watched) of the otter's attention span when the object at the end of its gaze declines to move. This felt about right. Abruptly, and with two leisurely strides, it was back in the water, swimming away downstream, running the bank, swimming, running, in and out of the water with the same unbroken fluency. Then it cut away from the bank, crossed the dark sand of the open shore at a leisurely, hunch-backed lope and, without pause or backward glance, nosed into the first of the waves, porpoised twice in deeper water and was gone.

*

Not all otters are thirled to Hebridean shores. In the heart of what I think of as my writer's home territory, where Lowland and Highland collide around the southernmost mountains and more or less equidistant from the east and west coasts of mainland Scotland, there is a watershed where I walk often. A lochan lies there beneath wooded hills and shines like a brooch on a crumpled cloak of glacial moraine and old oakwood. On a May morning with the sun newly roused, it is a place packed with nature's possibilities. Better than the metaphor of the brooch is the notion of the lochan as an eye, the landscape's watcher, commanding a view of miles of high country. But I think of it in that way only because Henry David Thoreau taught me to. That founding father of America's admirable and enviable nature-writing tradition wrote in *Walden*: "A lake is the landscape's most beautiful and expressive feature. It is earth's eye, looking into which the beholder measures the depth of his own nature."

It is one of those original thoughts that changed forever the way I look at a watersheet, and Gavin Maxwell's "at the edge of the ocean he stands on the brink of his own unconscious" echoes the sentiment. Over the years that I have been accustomed to walking up to the lochan in every season and at every hour of the day (and a few of the night), I have acquired a good measure of the depth of my own nature. The otter's nature there, however, has proved more elusive.

Unlike the otter of the islands, which is unfazed by daylight, in the landlocked heartlands of the watershed the otter is mostly a haunter of dusk and dawn and the hours in between. I know now where it comes from and where it goes, for it advertises its travels as legibly as a spread map. It climbs up from the burn which it has followed upstream from the river half a mile away, squirts through the mesh of an old stock fence (see its flattened trail through the tussocks), contours across the rough ground to a crossroads with a fox-roe-deer-pine-marten path where it pauses to spraint, and from there it drops down a short, steep ramp to the south shore of the lochan. There it skirts a big rock discarded by a glacier and a favourite perch for buzzards, owls, merlins, kestrels. And a young, wandering sea eagle roosted nearby for a week in that rambling oak on the steep slope of the east bank. It littered the ground beneath the tree with pellets the size of my fist.

There is another sprainting place at the edge of the water, just beyond a perfectly formed grass-walled-and-roofed tunnel one otter wide and a yard long. I have an unfulfilled ambition to see the otter negotiate that tunnel for which it was sole architect and engineer. In winter, snow consolidates the tunnel even more, and the ramp becomes one of several otter slides around the watershed. And when snow lies on the frozen surface of the lochan, footprints confirm the otter's preferred route across to the far side where it hauls out by a narrow outflow. Here it spraints again on the bank before squirming down the outflow that feeds into a second smaller and more overgrown lochan that, in turn, seeps into a reed bed where the otter finally covers its tracks and heads to God-knows-where.

It avoids the lochan on its return journey, preferring a long meander back down the burn to the river. In the snow, or in patches of wet mud near the lochan, all otter footprints head north, but in sandy nooks where the burn bends they head both north and south. There is a certain amount that can be read about the otter, then, but despite many, many hours at the lochan and following my idea of the otter's regular route, I have never seen one there, and it could be that it is reserved for the dead of night. The mystery endures, a state of affairs I find reassuring.

But I do see otters on the river, especially in its quieter floodplain reaches. There is a level stretch of bank topped by a mile of trees – alders, willow and birch mostly. The slow, gnawing river toys with the roots. A wide and shallow heap of sediment below the bank is laced every morning with the five-toed, webbed tracks of dead-of-night otters. I was their near neighbour for a while. One early March dawn I saw the bitch imprinting the frosted grass. Her spoor was indistinct footprints and a distinct furrow left by her tail. She shouldered aside a ground mist. Her side-on shape was low and slender, a purposeful gait along the top of the bank. In profile her head was long and narrow, her fur was water-slicked and darkened, off-white under her chin and down her front. Her identity card.

She stopped, turned her head to stare at me where I leaned against a tree. She knew me, or rather she was familiar with my shape, my scent, my presence. From nose to tail-tip she was a yard and a half long. (Her mate, the dog otter was a foot longer, heftier, wore a forehead scar. He'd been around. He wore no white. Mostly he kept his distance.) She walked on, curved tightly down to her left, descended the bank by a path of bare earth, her path. At the foot was a sprawl of roots. Something, some signal I missed, moved between her and the roots, for two cubs about half her size emerged to meet her. One had a white front and one did not. If there was a greeting, I missed that too. There was no fuss. They eased into the water as if the river waited for them. The bitch dived among bubbles; the cubs swam behind her on the surface. The mist closed in behind them.

I know otters occasionally travel up to the lochan at least two at a time because sometimes in past winters the snow showed two sets of meandering tracks and one was invariably bigger than the other. I want to know if it was the dog and the bitch, or the bitch with a well-grown cub, or two well-grown cubs exploring independently, or something else I haven't thought of.

Why do I want to know these things? Two reasons. One is simply to write them down, for my trade is that of a writer and I wander among wild places in search of their secrets to try and write them down. The second reason is more complicated but it has to do with Thoreau's observation about the beholder measuring the depths of his own nature. I do a lot of beholding. There is no better time to behold than a May morning or evening, when it seems as if all nature's tribes are on the move at once and giving voice, and the earlier the morning and the later the evening, the more accessible are their secrets. As Seton Gordon put it: "... the spirit of the high and lonely places revealed herself ..." Writing down the spirit of the high and lonely places, then, is my day job, my night job too, for that matter. Such an abstract idea becomes more tangible in places when the beholder's relationship with nature is an intimate one, the result of going again and again and over years, and so acquire a sense of nature's prevailing patterns. Everything I gather from familiar landscapes is more precious as a beholder, as a writer, because my own presence in such landscapes is also a part of the pattern, and I reclaim the ancient right of my own species to be part of nature myself.

There was a May morning on the watershed, and an otter had been there not long before me, for a spraint by the lochan was wet and glistening and fresh. Was the otter still there? Using the lie of the land I made a circuit of the loch – without showing myself to anything on the surface or the banks – and climbed up a rock twenty or thirty feet above the water and settled there with a view over the lochan, the moraines and beyond to the forest, to near and distant hills. Over two hours, I saw the following:

The nesting pair of Canada geese (a direct link with Thoreau, who mentions them specifically in *Walden*); a heron that flew in from the south and worked the shore and shallows from the shadow of what I now think of as the sea eagle oak; a water vole (the first I've ever seen there); three different male little grebes (I know the three messy nests hidden in shoreline vegetation); a green woodpecker flying in shallow bounces; a male cuckoo calling on a wire; a roebuck barking in a stand of willows; two mute swans flying north (for me, still the most heart-stirring sight and sound in all nature); an osprey with a fish for a lowered undercarriage (it nests on a dead birch tree left standing in an area of clear-felled spruces); skylarks; tree pipits; a male redstart; reed buntings; a sun-burnished red fox nosing along an old stone dyke; and the resident male buzzard quartering his territory (and he can measure the depths of his own nature by beholding the lochan from high overhead … my viewpoint on the rock was very good, his was much better).

If the otter was still around, it didn't show. After two hours on the rock, I left for a late breakfast. I was buoyant with the sensations and encounters of nature's morning, but the otter insinuated a familiar sliver of disappointment, one more near miss. I would be back at the rock in the late evening, for such is the nature of the watershed beholder.

*

Shetland and I got on well together from the first moment of the first day. That would have been in 1990 when I began working on a book called *Shetland – Land of the Ocean* with photographer and publisher Colin Baxter. Colin was a generous supporter of my early nature-writing years, and the Shetland book would be the high water mark of our collaborations.

The light floored me. There is the singular charm of island light, there is a further embellishment of northern light, and then there is the light of northern islands, which unites the two and elevates light into something like a state of grace. Why wouldn't otters be there?

The Shetland I truly fell for was the island of Yell, right in the middle of the archipelago. In particular, there was an early April week in a tiny caravan a few yards above the high tide at Mid Yell Voe, where I lingered over evening meals for one, watching otters and eider ducks from the window by the table. Wherever you look seawards from Yell, and especially if you have acquired a little bit of height, the view is of other islands and the intervening scraps of ocean and the interplay of sunlight and shadow, wind and rain and rainbows. And come late May and June the light was boundless (Sibelius in my head day after day), and nightfall was little more than an hour of gloaming.

The best of it all was Ness of Galtagarth. We met for the first time one cold and sunlit morning of that early April week. It is a small and flat island umbilically linked to the rest of Yell by a tombolo. Its outer shore is a treachery of rounded and knife-edged boulders coated with seaweed, all of which spills seawards from an eroding peat bank. The peat, where it meets the rock, overhangs or crumbles into a more or less continuous alleyway one otter wide.

Shetland is a benevolent host to otters. There are hundreds of miles of untrampled coastline and tempting inshore waters stuffed with fish and crabs and other delights. It was here in 1983 that wildlife cameraman Hugh Miles broke new ground with a remarkable television film called *The Track of the Wild Otter.* I was a newspaper journalist in Edinburgh at the time, nurturing dreams of writing about nature for a living. That film was an electrifying jolt to my ambitions, a work of insight and beauty.

In half an hour I found my first otter. It was fifty yards out and swimming parallel to the shore, deploying that purposeful porpoising technique of an otter on the march. For as long as the otter's direction of travel and the essentially curved nature of the shore permitted, I kept pace with it, running and scrambling (and falling) while it was underwater, crouching and freezing when it surfaced. Only the otter was dignified in its movements. I was trying too hard to keep the otter in sight as the shore curved away from its line of travel, instead of paying attention to where I was putting my feet, and to learning something of the lie of the land and its otter-watching possibilities. As a result, I failed to see what I should have seen, and so squandered an opportunity to watch an otter at very close quarters.

Even as the swimming otter disappeared from view, I was suddenly and woefully belatedly aware of a second otter. It was a large, gingery dog otter curled up and dozing in the sun five paces in front of me. In the same moment that I registered the rhythmical rise and fall of its flank, the edge of the peat bank collapsed under my left boot. The disturbance was not loud, but it didn't have to be to gatecrash an otter's mid-morning doze. It awoke, of course, uncurled and took the twenty yards of shoreline rocks at a flat-out blur, diving into the water without pause and surfacing twenty yards further out. Only from that sanctuary did it turn to scrutinise the intruder. It dived again and was gone.

I considered its sprint across those rocks, the nature of the terrain and the sure-footed ease I had just witnessed. It was, I decided, comparable to me covering a hundred metres of the Cuillin Ridge in ten seconds. From a sleeping start.

Thereafter, I walked with more consideration of my surroundings, noting a great deal of evidence of otters all around the shore, but I had ridden my luck, and saw no more. Instead, there was a pair of whimbrels that shrieked drily, stepped up from the shingle and hung on the wind like coat hangers for a moment then wheeled away across the voe.

The next day I had to leave Yell and it snowed: otter tracks in white at the edge of the ocean.

A Long Wait in the Wind

Lines written on the Braer disaster, Quendale Bay, Shetland, January 1993

It has been a long wait
in the wind, that ill-at-ease
wind of change. Now fear
is laid aside to deal dully with disaster.
But at least we *knew*
about the wait, the wait
and the warning and the wind.
The otters and the birds
knew only the wind.

Ever since our glad hand beckoned
oil ashore at Sullom Voe
we began to wait for its gatecrash
on some wild and unprepared tract
a reckoning behind our backs. On an island
you can only face one shore at a time.

Today the reckoning
is fastened to Quendale Bay
like a peninsula
and the warning ones were right:
the oil has not come ashore
at Sullom Voe.

The wind has done this.
The waiting ones said it would
for the wind permits no lethargies of the soul
for the Shetlander and varies
only in the degrees of its withering assault.

Otter

Life here is a courageous compliance bowing
to the overlordship of winds,
mourning and singing to their whims.
Today we mourn. One bright tomorrow
on Ronas Hill, the wind
will eddy the land in song
and we will sing too and briefly forget
forget today and the new waiting
which by then will have begun.

Besides, all Shetland's story
is wrought by winds of change.
This ill-at-ease wind bore gifts
– jobs, roads, ferries,
social vigour, brimming coffers –
and stemmed that cancerous flow
– south! south! – of our children.
Why then should there not be a price?

And at least we knew
about the wait
the wait the warning and the wind
But oh! if only
we could have warned the fish
the birds the seals and the otters

and our lovely land.

The Wind That Sulks

Lines written a year after the event

Nature has ripped the headlines from her.
She's yesterday's news
Broken sunken shrunken to sea level.
The world has packed and gone to stare
at someone else's *Braer.*

Now I should go back
now the watcher tides have ebbed
and left behind the battened down islanders.
I was absent for the wounding
but I should be there for the healing
after the heroics
enduring
aligned with the stoics.

Besides I too have grieved.
Distance salts the wounds of others
in my mind – Shetland and Shetlander,
flier and swimmer
the clean air grown black
the sea gone deadly slack.

But expert voices cried
"The wind has healed!"
while silent Shetland waits
and fears the unforgiving unrevealed hand
the wind may play
the unpredicted price to pay.
For every enemy the islands ever knew
who burned and warred
and reefed the coasts in hulks
Shetland only ever learned to fear
The wind that sulks.

Beaver

The River Earn in Perthshire, a windless mid-October noontide. It was prime autumn in that heartland terrain of many big trees strutting their prime autumn stuff, yet the day had plunged into a quagmire of gloom. A smirr drenched every piece and particle of land and air. The day had a soundtrack, no less incessant: the throb of red deer stags unseen within the shroud of cloud that wrapped the hills to within a hundred feet of the riverbanks.

For me, this is where Scotland's beaver adventure began. Their spoor has been reconfiguring these banks and surrounding waters throughout this century. It seems to me they enjoy such days as this one. Textbooks will tell you that they are creatures of dawn and dusk and darkness, and mostly they are. But the textbooks don't tell you that a noon-tide like this one is not so different from a dawn or a dusk and that sometimes beavers will behave as if it *were* dawn or dusk. The gloom renders them all but invisible, for they are the same grey shades as the day itself, and besides, humans are more or less absent. So the beavers can be up and doing in the middle of the day, safe from all the usual sources of daylight disturbance, right? Not quite.

I have known the River Earn for most of my life. It emerges fully formed out of Loch Earn and flows east to meet the Tay near Perth, and the Tay has coursed through my entire life. I grew up on its banks and it is forever luring me back from every corner of Scotland and far beyond. The nature writer in me was delighted when beavers colonised the Earn before the official story of their proposed reintroduction had begun, and I have followed their progress hereabouts ever since. No sooner had they begun to make the changes they like to make to a landscape when they move in than I began seeing otters. Fact: otters like the company of beavers and seem to seek it out.

This intrigues. In Scotland, otters had not lived alongside beavers for around 400 years when this twenty-first century reintroduction began. Yet it has taken them no time to reconvene a historic relationship. This suggests that race memory is indestructible. And that the race of otters has always known there are advantages to be gained from being around the race of beavers. It is demonstrably true in North America, and it is true in Western Europe. In Scotland the two species have simply taken up where they left off.

So I was watching with some fascination what looked like a stash of fallen leaves over by the far bank. I knew from repeated visits that the leaves constituted a new addition to the local beaver architecture, for they were not fallen leaves at all but harvested leaves – beaver-harvested leaves. Their stems were still attached to long, skinny twigs of more-or-less uniform length. I knew too that they were piled against a slowly subsiding remnant of what had been a small dam.

And there had just been an unusual movement at the heart of the stash: it had just heaved upwards and subsided again.

Rational thinking suggested a beaver was at work just below the surface. I already suspected that the dam had originally provided tranquil water behind it for an underwater entrance to a burrowed bank-side lodge, which would be the preferred accommodation on such a turbulent river where a timber-built lodge would succumb repeatedly to spates. It was possible that the slowly decomposing dam still provided that service, that even now the beaver was moving the stash of leaves to an underwater larder, that although it was the middle of the day the low light offered cover enough for the beaver to be at work on the river. I fully expected it to appear at any moment.

No sooner had the thought formed than the pile of leaves burst apart. Long stems of autumn leaves were hurled in every direction. Then the source of the explosion powered through the chaos at a steep upward trajectory until it was almost completely out of the water, and only when it curved back towards the surface of the water in a monumental splashdown did the soundtrack catch up with the spectacle. When the mayhem subsided, an otter was swimming in a wide midstream arc. Almost at once and in complete silence, a beaver materialised on the surface and began edging back and forward, upstream and downstream, a patrolling sentry intent on denying the otter a second opportunity to inflict turmoil on the beaver's underworld before it had been discouraged with such dramatic effect. The tension between the two animals was unmistakable. For the next minute they confronted each other without making contact, without giving way and with no sound but the river's easy speech. A prelude to further hostilities? Or a necessary striking of final postures so that neither would lose face?

The quiet was shattered by the bellow of a red deer stag, much closer and much lower down the hillside than anything I had heard that morning. Neither otter nor beaver reacted to the sound. They would know its meaning and know that it presented neither threat nor food source, so why trouble? Mercifully, I am not equipped with such indifference. My mind's eye lingered up there just inside the loose coils of low cloud that slipped further and further down the hillside as the morning advanced. The stag was not alone; if anything, the answering roar was closer. I imagined their ritualised strut, known as "parallel walking", the precursor to the moment where physical challenge is accepted or declined. What was going on in the water had an element of ritual stand-off and appraisal too, and I wondered where else in all the wild world there might be another human participating by way of a dead-still presence in the simultaneous and tension-laden moments of three creatures as diverse as otter, beaver and stag. Right time, right place – there is nothing at all more priceless in a nature writer's life.

The finale to the impasse on the river was disappointingly prosaic. The beaver turned its back on the otter and began retrieving what it could of the scattered leaves and ferrying them back to the disordered remnants of the original pile. The otter crossed the river to my bank and left the water by a track through trees and thick undergrowth that I had noticed before, but which I assumed was a beaver track. In truth, there is no reason why they would not both use it, and quite possibly they also share it with badger and fox and deer coming to the river to drink. The otter paused at the top of the bank, one forepaw raised, and looked back to where the beaver was still gathering and reordering the scattered foliage, swimming downstream and collecting it in substantial mouthfuls as it turned back into the current. Back at the site of the original stash, it piled the recovered stems against the quiet side of the dam, so that they were out of the current and formed a compact raft, the bottom of which may have rested on part of the dam. Then it swam back out into the open river and began patrolling the outer edge of the dam again while the otter still watched.

Perhaps the otter saw this as a new challenge. It retraced its steps to the water's edge, where it paused again. The beaver met this gesture (if gesture is what it was) by swimming straight towards the otter, turning a yard away then smashing the leathery paddle of its tail onto the surface and disappearing in the same instant. The otter, which must have seen beaver indignation before, turned its back, imparting the sense of a shrug, and walked away along the top of the bank, keeping a certain distance between itself and the river – the required discretion that is the better part of valour.

Mostly, otters and beavers put up with each other because they have no choice, and because out-and-out hostility is not in their interests, given that both are well armed with teeth and powerful jaws. But only otters have anything to gain from the relationship. As far as I can see, beavers gain nothing from proximity to otters. The beaver is a vegetarian, the otter a carnivore. Newly emerged beaver kits are certainly vulnerable to otters, and otters can enter beaver lodges the same way beavers do. Tension is highest between the species when kitts are around.

There is no corresponding threat from beavers to otter cubs. The other bonus for otters is that they like what beavers do, the way they manipulate water. For example, on this stretch of the Earn the beavers dug out a canal parallel to the river, a canal the river replenishes whenever the water level rises. Beavers dammed the downstream end of the canal and dug out a deep pool there. Young fish like the sheltered nature of the canal and the pool and sometimes larger fish rest up there too, so it is hardly surprising that otters are regular visitors.

*

My first beaver was this. A shudder went through the surface of the Earn. Something was untoward near the far bank where water so tranquil it was almost at a standstill was suddenly beset by shallow corrugations advancing *upstream*; and in a pre-dawn gloom energised by fitful mist, there was an eerie cast to the troubled surface. The disturbance sprawled out into the river in ever diminishing troughs until they reached that critical point in midstream where the current was too strong and their outer edges were bent back and dissolved. Yet something must have generated the original disturbance, given it impetus and then sustenance so that it flowed upstream in the quiet waters of the far bank. I was startled into a stillness of my own. The thing to do now, I told myself, is nothing at all. I am particularly good at doing nothing at all. It is a gift that serves a nature writer well, and although I can take no credit for it – for I appear to have been born with it – I nurture it by constant practice. This was a moment for watchful stillness, so I did nothing at all.

Then a tree started to swim towards me.

It had to be swimming rather than just floating because it, too, was moving upstream against the tug of the current. It was not a whole tree but a substantial part of a small one, and with foliage trailing out into midstream. It stood to reason that it must have a source of propulsion, otherwise it would turn in its own length and float away downstream, where, a few miles further on, it would enter the Tay, pick up speed, blur past Newburgh, Dundee and by nightfall or daybreak be somewhere out by the Bell Rock lighthouse. Instead of that it had covered twenty upstream yards in about half a minute, and as it drew level with me I realised that a curious bulge that deformed the otherwise straight and slender trunk was the top half of the head of a swimming beaver. At that point in my constantly evolving relationship with nature, I had never seen the head of a swimming wild beaver before, with or without a tree attached. In the greater scheme of things, this was quite a moment.

Then I saw a tree standing right at the water's edge with a bite out of it. People who live near beavers are all too aware of them even though they rarely see them: the trees bear the scars, or they disappear from their accustomed stances and suddenly water flows where they were accustomed to stand. And here was my first tree with a bite out of it. Nearby was an unbitten tree higher up the bank from the bitten tree, and as I wore tree-coloured clothes I sat there and put my back to it. But because this was new to me, I was tense when I wanted to be calm. Tension transmits itself to many animals. Troubled by this state of mind, I executed an awkward sidestep. My camera, which I had slung over one shoulder, slipped off and bounced against tree bark. It was not a loud sound, and I caught the strap. But there was an immediate muffled explosion behind the bitten tree, and a loose branch clattered against the roots and bounced into shallow water. A hefty, dark grey-brown and bluntly rounded shape leapt into the river, followed by a startlingly loud splash from what I now know to be a beaver tail slapping the surface of the water as it dived. In the process, it advertised my presence to every beaver and every other creature along several hundred yards of river. The noise was extraordinary. There is a landmark in beaver literature, a Canadian book called *Castorologia*, by Horace T. Martin, published in 1892. It had this to say about the beaver's tail:

It is nearly flat, broad and straight, and covered with horny scales of a lustrous black. Its principal uses are to elevate or depress the head while swimming, to turn the body and vary its direction, and to assist the animal in diving. When alarmed in his pond, particularly at night, he immediately dives, in doing which the posterior part of his body is thrown out of the water, and as he descends head foremost, the tail is brought down upon the surface of the water with a heavy stroke, and deep below it with a plunge. It is capable of diagonal movement from side to side...and also of assuming a near vertical position. He is able to turn his tail under him and to sit on it, or to use it extended behind him as prop when sitting on his hind feet.

I looked around at a wide oasis of purposefully rearranged river water. That oasis was designed, engineered, project-managed and built with beaver hands and feet, and beaver teeth. Likewise the dam that held it all in place, likewise the lodge with its air vent, watergate and complex of living spaces and larders. Likewise the canals that radiated from riverbank into woodland: these offered fast escape from shoreline wood to the safety of deep water, escape from such historic threats as wolves and wolverines that must still exist in the race memory of twenty-first-century Scottish beavers. Even though neither wolf nor wolverine torment the beavers of Perthshire, both species are still active in mainland Europe, and even though there is no historic evidence of wolverine here, and the wolf has been gone for at least 200 years, who knows when the people will reintroduce the wolves, and whether legally or illegally, and who is going to tell the beavers?

So beavers heed instinct and their architecture and engineering skills include canal building. More than a hundred years ago now, the American writer and naturalist Ernest Thompson Seton wrote that "the beaver was the original inventor of reinforced concrete. He has used it for a million years, in the form of mud mixed with sticks and stones." And the architectural magician that is Frank Gehry invented the term "liquid architecture" to describe his process. "It's like jazz," he explained. "You improvise, you work together, you play off each other, you make something ..." Beavers build landscapes from scratch and from water that flows and timber that grows in the wrong place, and all life is improvised liquid architecture. Do you suppose Frank Gehry ever watched beavers?

*

In the course of writing a handful of books about a single species – *Waters of the Wild Swan* (Cape, 1992), *Badgers on the Highland Edge* (Cape, 1994), *The Last*

Wolf (Birlinn, 2010), *The Eagle's Way* (Saraband, 2014) – there was a common element to the fieldwork that underpinned them all. By concentrating on one creature, you find yourself drawn into the lives of every other creature with which it interacts and every other creature with which it shares its landscape. Nothing in nature lives and works in complete isolation. It has proved no less true of beavers than it was with any of the others. It became apparent during my first few visits to that stretch of the Earn that in addition to such essentially river-thirled creatures as herons, dippers, kingfishers, sandpipers, salmon, trout and otters, I would also be seeing a lot of red kites. I was not aware of any relationship between kite and beaver, but on my very first afternoon at the river, I heard a pair of kites calling within half an hour as they crossed the river a hundred feet up. They have in common with beavers that they were rendered extinct in Scotland and have been reintroduced. The culprits were the usual suspects – the Victorian sporting estates, the Victorian egg-collecting mania and the Victorian enthusiasm for killing things to stuff and display in glass cases. The killing still goes on, for both red kite and beaver, despite the highest level of legal protection, and is surely as deeply ingrained in the DNA of the reintroduced beaver as it is in the DNA of the reintroduced red kite. That is the nature of the relationship between them.

Beaver

In late summer when I first came to look for beavers on the river, it was mostly in the deep shadow of the well-wooded canopy, and only a narrow blue furrow of sky that followed the course of the river let in much light. But it was there that I would see and hear fragmented moments of kite flight. At first, I was absorbed in the beavers' constantly evolving timber operations, the innumerable questions, the infrequent glimpses of the critters themselves – their strangeness in my eyes. The place had an introverting, captivating ambience. I would arrive discreetly, inspect the various hives of activity within the space of a couple of hundred yards of riverbank, then sit and wait for something to watch. And every now and then, the sky would call down to me through the gap in the canopy and there was a kite, or a pair of kites, mocking my willing incarceration in the shadows, while they flirted with wind and sunlight.

It was late autumn the day I first explored upstream. There had been a hard frost, and ice had nibbled at the shallows. The last bars of the anthem of the red deer rut still rumbled down the hillsides to the south. I walked out of the trees and into much more open country, and within minutes there were three buzzards wheeling and side-slipping, diving and soaring, and the excited edge of their calls cut brightly through the clear, still air. And with them were four red kites, and their keener and giddier voices laced the melee. This tumbleweed of birds drifted northwards. The red kite is a slender, leisurely, airy waltzer, and a buzzard is two-thirds of the way to being eagle, with many of the eagle's traits. I am guessing now, but this looked much more like stuff-strutting than dog-fighting, point-scoring perhaps, striving for status. From time to time a buzzard would climb above the kites and attempt to dive down through them, and each time the kites split in four different directions, a last-gasp waft of guile so that the buzzard fell through the hole in the doughnut.

Gradually, a pattern emerged. The kites seemed to be on the move from east to west, but the buzzards seemed hell-bent on turning them north, or at least somewhere north of west. Each time the kites reunited after a buzzard dive they started west again, but one buzzard after another would mob them from above, below and behind, and the morass of birds would edge a little more towards the distant hills in the north. It was as if the kites were an immovable impediment strewn across the buzzards' road north and must be moved aside like a snowplough moves snow. How long this might have lasted is anyone's guess, but I foresaw its denouement a second or two before it actually happened. I was suddenly aware of another bird in the glasses much higher than the group I was watching. Then there was another one by its side, then another, then three more, then ... so I shifted the focus of the binoculars onto this higher group, and I saw that there was a second tier of birds, that there were about forty of them, that they were moving west, and that they were all red kites. Suddenly the buzzards were drifting away to the north and the four lower kites amalgamated seamlessly into these higher squadrons and their suddenly silent bandwagon rolled on.

*

A string of clear nights either side of a full moon suggested that beavers by moonlight might be a good idea. The same stretch of river where I had watched the kites looked promising, not least because the river parted around a raised bank of shingle to make a small island of it, and I had heard beavers are drawn to natural islands. So I walked out into the first of the open fields where the moonlight flooded the land and my moonshadow leapt into life. The river looped north in a long curve. A shrub-darkened burn oozed down the side of the field, and although I was as moonlit as anything else out there, my shape would be against the darkness of shrubs and clusters of small trees, and that might diminish my impact on the landscape among the watching night eyes, and the mutter of the burn might deaden my footfall. Beavers had left their signature on the few standing trees along the bank, which further encouraged me. Even if nothing else happened, it was a mesmeric night to be out.

A single hawthorn bush about my own height was handily placed and might just serve to break up my silhouette. Then something out on the shingle moved a few inches, before sliding back into position, an odd enough movement to demand a second look. What had moved was a piece of wood, a long thin piece of birchwood, part of which was violent white in the moonlight where the bark had been peeled. It leaned up awkwardly at a shallow angle from its downstream end lying in the water, and at the far end a beaver was sitting on its back legs with its tail splayed out behind and flat on the stones, and in its forefeet was a strip of peeled bark which it was eating in an attitude of deep concentration. In the moonlight.

It was the best, the clearest, the most captivating, the most memorable view of a beaver I had had, and it still is. At that point, I had been working on my beaver researches for about a year, and I was still unreconciled to the often hemmed-in, half-lit world they occupied, and more than once I had been reminded of how, at the lowest points of watching badgers, it had been forcibly impressed on me that I didn't much care for black woods at night. There had come a defining moment when I was writing *Badgers on the Highland Edge* that changed everything, for I had got lucky. And now, I had just got lucky again, and that singular beaver poised in midstream in the full glare of the all-but-full moon, peeling back a loose end of bark as if it was banana peel, reached across the water and the intervening airspace and ensnared me for a willing conscript to its cause.

*

The Earn was not my first beaver water. The Yukon was. In 1998 I was invited by BBC Natural History Unit radio producer Grant Sonnex to make two half-hour programmes about the relationship between people and wilderness – in Alaska. For a nature writer like me, based in Scotland, the project was life-changing. Its consequences are forever creeping into my writing even now.

At my request, we had made a diversion to find trumpeter swans (my passion for swans has endured for more than half my life). A biologist called Dave took us to a lake in the Yukon valley near the Alaska–Canada border, a lake where trumpeters were nesting. We had to drive a few miles, then walk a few. From his campervan window we saw unaccustomed movement 200 yards from the road. Big, slow movement. My first grizzly bear, and it was berry picking. We stopped. It vanished. How does something that size vanish? We waited. The bear crashed through roadside vegetation and crossed the road fifty yards in front of us. It stopped on the far side, stared at the vehicle, then ambled away up a roadside bank and disappeared into forest. Dave showed us the footprints. I have big hands, goalkeeping hands. The footprints were the size of goalkeeping hands. On the same bank of bare earth were the prints of wolf and moose. Dave said: "Welcome to the wilderness, Jim."

Dave's first line of defence against bears was his dog, a three-legged mutt which would know about their proximity long before we did, or at least long enough to make a difference. But I was thinking: "Why would we not want to meet a bear?" Fear of wild animals has never been a part of my make-up (although I have met a handful of people I would run a mile from), and I admit to a degree of disappointment when I encounter it in others.

We walked in forest, but forest unlike any other I had ever seen. I passed a tree that appeared to have been felled at knee-height, but not by axe or passing gale. The stump ended in a meticulously curved point like a pencil, and the "sharpened" portion was patterned all over with small indented patches. I recognised it for what it was only from a hundred different book and magazine photographs. Beaver reintroduction in Scotland was still a decade away.

"Is this beaver?"

"Yep."

"Where is the trunk?"

"Broken into chunks and ferried to the lake to build lodges and dams."

"Ferried?"

"Sure. You just stepped over his canal."

"*His* canal? Whose?"

"Beaver's."

What looked like a rough ditch that hissed agreeably with light rain was my first beaver-designed canal. It became clear more or less at once, standing there and looking round, really *looking*, that it was part of a network. It led directly to a broad pool.

"The pool?"

"Also beaver. There's a curved dam on the far side that holds the water there, and an outlet that goes all the way down to the shore. Little fish in it too. Not that they eat fish, but plenty of things that do eat fish catch them there; thing about beavers is they're always putting food in the mouths of other critters."

That was the first, but by no means the last time, that I would hear that argument, and as my writing became deeply involved in the Scottish beaver reintroduction programme in the years to come, I would deploy it myself, using Dave's words.

More and more pointed stumps appeared, some with felled trunks nearby or even still attached, but almost every fallen trunk was stripped of branches and foliage and bark. There were also many trees that beavers had gnawed most of the way through then abandoned. Dave explained that these "snags" – standing deadwood – were perfect for wood-burrowing bugs and woodpeckers; that fallen deadwood breaks down and increases the fertility of the forest floor, fertility that creates openings for new plants, new trees; and in the process they create new opportunities "for water to do its thing … they create havoc then they leave it, and nature makes a garden of it, because nature has time."

And I would also deploy that argument, and make more of it, because of the demonstrable rightness of what I saw that day, and what I was taught. In retrospect, the hours with Dave Mossop have the feel of an ecology masterclass.

"So the trumpeter swans have beavers for neighbours?"

"Yup. I guess they know each other pretty well. And sometimes it's the other way round and the beavers have the swans for neighbours: I've heard of swans that built a nest on a beaver dam."

"Why?"

"Dunno why. Maybe out along some of these boggy shores it's the only solid thing they can find to build on."

So that was how beavers entered my life, deep in the Yukon where Canada and Alaska seep seamlessly into each other. That was how they first commended themselves to me because of their accomplishments in what is surely the ultimate form of architecture, for the architects not only design and build, but also select their own raw materials, engineer the means to move them from source to building site, physically move them, then move in. All that, and they are friends and neighbours of the world's largest swans.

If I say that the eventual distant appearance of the swans was mildly anti-climactic, its demotion from the be-all-and-end-all I was havering about over breakfast was simply because of where it cropped up in the day's order of events. A beaver-managed waterworld on such a scale was a profoundly impressive introduction, an invaluable lesson in the art of wilderness-in-the-making.

And then there was the lake and the swans (and they were huge: a big cob has a ten-foot wingspan), two adults and four dowdy cygnets. Our view from a few hundred yards away was constantly interrupted by trees as the birds swam around, feeding. I was wondering how close we might get when Dave's dog suddenly went nuts. He yipped and growled and bolted back to us, the fastest thing I had ever seen on three legs. His hair stood on end. Then Dave's voice:

"Holy Toledo! Bear bed!"

"Bear bed?"

"Grizzly makes a day-bed where he lies up. Here."

On the ground was a rough, circular scrape five or six feet across and a deep duvet of grass and ferns, the most innocuous-looking thing in the forest, if you don't know its meaning. Once you do know its meaning, you get to thinking about who made the bed and who's been cat-napping there. Dave looked at the bear bed and at his dog.

"I don't like this," he said.

"You think the bear is still around?"

"I think the dog thinks so. Could be. Not worth the risk. I think a strategic withdrawal is called for."

"Bugger."

On the way back, I took the trouble to notice when I stepped over a beaver canal, to admire the workmanship that chimed perfectly with a true wilderness landscape. If it was a frustrating end to the swan expedition, it was a perfectly distilled shorthand introduction to that extraordinary country. The beavers I have been watching on the River Earn have kingfishers and dippers and otters and red kites for neighbours, and any of these can engross me for hours at a time. The beavers on the Yukon have the biggest swans in the world and grizzly bears and moose for neighbours, and for sure they will be harassed from time to time by wolves.

Badger

Once upon a time, a very unusual man became Secretary of the Bank of England. Why unusual? Because he wrote this: "There's no security or peace or tranquillity, except underground ... No builders, no tradesmen, no remarks passed on you by fellows looking over your wall, and above all, no weather."

They don't make Secretaries of the Bank of England like that anymore. Most people don't know the names of the various Secretaries of the Bank of England but millions know the name of this one, but not because he was Secretary of the Bank of England. He was Kenneth Grahame and he wrote *The Wind in the Willows*. And he put the words quoted above into the mouth of The Badger. A badger emerges from its underground sett warily, often after a few false starts, and with an air of reluctance. I have no idea how competent Kenneth Grahame was as Secretary of the Bank of England, but he knew badgers.

I came to them late. When my book *Badgers on the Highland Edge* was published (Jonathan Cape, 1994), it was no profound authority on the species. Rather, it was a book about finding out about badgers, an adventure in discovery. It's difficult to explain now why it took me so long to become a badger watcher, although some kind of psychological barrier perhaps infiltrated my mind after the discovery of my very first badger and festered there for decades. I was a teenager with a bike and the wild world was a barely prised oyster crammed with pearls, but my first badger was not one of these. It floated face-down in the pond of a derelict mill and I lifted it out by the scruff of the neck. It was as shapeless as a bad cushion, for it had been smashed and wounded many times and what I held was its dumped corpse. A white horde of maggots writhed in its sodden fur. I dropped it back where I had found it and was at once helplessly sick.

After several minutes bent double in the bracken, I straightened up to find the black, unblinking eye of a robin watching me side-headed from a fence-post a yard away. It flew down onto the badger corpse, deftly plundered a beakful of maggots, then perched again on the fencepost just long enough for me to see that they still writhed. By the time the robin was cramming them into the tiny yellow yawns of its brood of nestlings in a bramble bush, I was being sick again. It was a bizarre introduction to badgers and it may explain a lot. Curiously, for years after, it put me off badgers rather than robins.

Time passes, we grow up, horizons widen. I would meet many badger enthusiasts over the years, and if they detected my lack of shared enthusiasm, none mentioned it. *Badgers on the Highland Edge* is a slender book, a tentative exploration, but it produced one extraordinary response. The great authority on the badger is Ernest Neal. His books *Badgers* (Blandford, 1977) and *The Natural History of Badgers* (Helm, 1986) are the internationally acknowledged authorities, the fruits of more than fifty years of study. I leaned on them heavily. In January, 1995, a letter arrived via my publisher. It began:

> *Dear Jim Crumley, I was given your badger book for Christmas. I just wanted to thank you for saying kind things about me and to say how much I enjoyed reading it. It took me right back to those early days – 1936 onwards – when any time I watched the badgers it was an adventure and a chance to add a tiny detail to the badger jigsaw about which so little was known then. Your studies were so refreshingly personal – a quest which rang a bell with me even after 50+ years of watching badgers ...*

It was signed: *Yours sincerely, Ernest G. Neil.*

I keep the letter inside the cover of my book. It still astounds me. The ghost of the old millpond was finally laid that day. Badgers crowded into my life.

*

The bracken had yet to turn. Lingering hints of summer warmed a September evening in the dense heart of a spruce plantation, flies as thick about my head as blossom on a May hawthorn. The sun was low and no shred of it penetrated the press of trees. Behind me were three hours of midge-tormented badger watching in which not a single badger showed. I was done. I headed for a cold beer on the way home. The way out lay along a forest ride where the bracken stopped but the grasses were waist-high and a wet ditch ran up the middle. In the grey half-light it was hard to see where the grass ended and the ditch began. But moving carefully between walls of trees while wearing the same spruce shades, there is always the chance of getting lucky, of catching something unawares.

Something had just rustled the grass.

Something that wasn't the wind.

Something that demanded silence, stillness.

By the time the grass stopped moving and then started again, every blade was in focus, and these slowly started to fall aside to accommodate a dark grey shape that paled and hardened into a badger head. A badger face was staring at me. I have seen many variations on the theme of that face in many different circumstances. It is a face I have never learned to take for granted. Nor have I learned to be anything other than impressed by its bearishness, particularly when it distinguishes the broad head of such a heavyweight boar. The half-light had a magnifying effect and brightened the white mask. Then he sat back. Just like that.

He did not run or panic or hide. He looked straight at me and sat back. Almost certainly he had sensed my presence before I sensed his, but given my dark and quiet passage through the evening forest and with the wind working against him, he had advanced and sat to see what his eyes might make of me. There is also the possibility that because of my repeated presence on his territory over the past two years he was accustomed to my shape and scent and it no longer troubled him because all I did was walk quietly and sit still. Now he sat and we faced each other across the beginning of the forest ride and somewhere between us a trickle of water muttered in the bottom of an unseen ditch.

I believe his sitting had a second purpose. When he first saw me, or rather when I first saw him looking at me (not necessarily the same thing), he was side-on to me and his profile was low to the ground. Then, just before he sat, he turned towards me, so that when he did sit back on his haunches his whole body was massed and curved behind his head, and being a heftily muscled beast, he suddenly looked three times the size of his side-on, low-slung self. The sitting was a pose designed to impress. It worked. He impressed me. Again.

He stared for perhaps twenty seconds then looked suddenly sideways, then back towards me. The grass moved again. The sow emerged. She padded over to him, parting the grass as she walked, leaving a padded-down track the width of herself behind her. She stopped behind him, half-hidden, peered round his shoulder at me, her head lower and flatter than his; the two white masks might have been the countenances of kindly ghosts. Then she turned and trotted to the forest edge and stepped inside the trees. He lingered a few seconds more, still staring, then grunted quietly and followed her.

I knew by now from repeated visits that they had two cubs, and I wondered if they were close by, and whether they were also in the grass and might respond to a summons from their parents. But there was no summons and the grass grew still. In the lull that followed, a woodcock hurtled up the ride and passed low overhead, coughing and squeaking, a curiously frog-voiced vocabulary for such an elegant bird. With the woodcock's passing, the forest acquired a new and muffling layer of evening. The quiet deepened and I held still, trusting to instinct. I was in a good position, there were badgers around. I had done the hard work. Now wait a little longer. Soft noises just inside the trees suggested they had not gone far.

I wondered if I might lure them back. Biologically, badgers are of the weasel tribe, the Mustelidae, and curiosity is a common trait of all that tribe. So I began to click my tongue and pop a finger against the inside of my mouth and whistle softly, anything that might rouse the curiosity of listening ears. And still there were soft rummaging sounds inside the edge of the trees. They were not leaving, but would they reappear? Just when I thought I was getting nowhere, the woodcock returned and its voice meshed with my noises and the boar's face was suddenly back and peering up from almost ground level beneath the lowest sweep of the spruce branches. Almost at once the sow was right beside him. Then the cubs. For no more than ten seconds all four faces gleamed garishly out of the forest at me. They put a smile on my face and it was all I could do to stifle a laugh.

By now I have watched badgers everywhere from a Knoydart mountainside to a mountain woodland in Balquhidder to Loch Leven in Kinross-shire to the shale bings of West Lothian and the coasts of Fife and Berwickshire, but nothing has charmed me so utterly as those ten seconds at the bottom of a spruce tree on the southernmost tip of the Trossachs. The circumstances had as much to do with it as anything. I have already mentioned my dislike of watching wildlife from hides or some kind of artificial set-up that persuades wildlife to linger. What delights me is this. The chance encounter that sheds light on how individual creatures do things out on their rounds, patrolling their territories, going about their business. And I find my own instincts best served when I can just be a discreet fragment of their world, a presence in their lives as they are in mine, for this is my chosen landscape too. My purpose is to encounter wildlife on its own terms – better, on terms that suit us both – for in such circumstances, that part of me which is still nature comes to the fore and dominates mind, eye, sensibility, and dignifies a human breast.

The badgers withdrew together.

I heard them shuffle away.

I listened until there was no more to hear.

Spell for Safe Badgers

Roof well timbered
with root of limber tree,
thatch of bracken.

Courage, stealth, health of cubs,
wealth of places to dig and scratch,
home patch lardered with worms,
peace, fleece of stars.

Badger

Wind far-carrying, cool marrying
of water and dark earth, dearth
of gun, gas, dog, trap, poison,
noisome men and their sour scents.
Otherwise, just leave us alone.

*

There is a scruffy little country lane I know that dives down into a dark and tousie wood as if it is ashamed of its own scruffiness, as well it might be. But it has always had one saving grace, and now I know it has two. The one I knew about before is that the wood accommodates a badger sett, never the easiest to watch because of its sheer size. And many of its forty or fifty entrances are close to the wood's roadside fence, and here and there the badgers have dug under the fence and come up in the roadside verge, spoil heaps spilling over into the lane.

The day I discovered the second saving grace I was walking the lane for no particular reason except that I had been working nearby and found myself with time to kill and it was a morning that held the smell and the aura of a new spring. I wouldn't be seeing adult badgers at midday in April, but I decided to check for signs of activity anyway. Besides, April is the cub month hereabouts, so I could always look for the patter of little footprints. You can stumble across unwary cubs at almost any time of the day. A well-honed sixth sense is among the most priceless assets of the nature watcher. The honing is the fruit of years, of patience, of ritual, of reworking a particular set of circumstances again and again and again, so that if something changes you sense it as readily as you might see or hear or touch or smell it on the wind. Almost all the cubs I have ever seen have been in daylight and well away from the core of the sett. So, instead of going into the wood, I went looking for the entrances to the under-the-fence tunnels on the roadside verge.

Two I remembered were overgrown and unused. But there were also two I had not remembered. They looked freshly dug, and there in the earth at the edge of the second one were some very small footprints indeed, too small for badger, and whatever the size of the badger, from a boar to a weeks-old cub, a badger footprint looks like a badger footprint and these did not. They belonged to what I now know to be the wood's second saving grace. I thought: "These look like …" and the thought remained unfinished because the face of the owner appeared in the mouth of the tunnel, saw me and vanished. I retreated, leaned against a tree, waited. I had good reason to believe the face would be back, and I wondered how long it might take. Three minutes maximum, I guessed. It took a minute and a half. A glimpse of white fur was followed by the two blackest eyes in the wildwood. These advanced none-too-cautiously into the daylight. In response to my clicking and popping routine, the creature advanced a yard into the lane, stopped, stood on its hind legs, stared a what's-your-problem stare. Pound for pound, or in this case ounce for ounce, is there anything more fearless on Earth than a weasel?

Its coat shone in a dapple of sunlight. It was sleek and skinny and it moved in ripples. It stood again and showed its teeth. But mostly it stared its black, unblinking stare. I thought of it then as the most dynamic of all our native mammals, the most packed with purpose and energy, the blithest athlete, the most confident in its own skin, the most undeferential beast on four legs this side of … this side of … nothing at all really.

It is also the nosiest creature in the wildwood, which is both part of its charm and, from time to time, the source of its downfall. Had I been a keeper with a gun – or whatever it is a keeper uses to reduce weasels to corpses on a barbed wire gibbet – that nosiness would have been a death sentence. As it was, I chatted away to the weasel and watched it come to six feet away from where I stood, sizing me up, all six inches of it nose-to-tail against my all-but-six-feet, obsessively determined to satisfy itself about the source of all that noise and, if necessary, to see it off. Just how close it would have dared I'll never know, for at that moment the ground began to shake and a tractor the size of a small farmhouse rounded the end of the wood and charged up the lane, towing a piece of machinery whose purpose quite baffled me. When it had been and gone, there was just an empty lane, a nasty smell of diesel and a thread of new footprints that disappeared deep inside the tunnel.

I have heard of all kinds of creatures sharing a badger sett with the badgers, and seen some of them – fox, rabbit, once a hare during a storm, once an otter – but I had not seen or heard of a weasel lodger. Ernest Neal had heard of it, but only on a casual and temporary basis. His Europe-wide list of "mammalian tenants of setts" in *The Natural History of Badgers* (Facts on File, 1986) includes wolf, porcupine, raccoon dog, pine marten, polecat and wildcat. So the weasel is in tow with uncompromising company, not to mention the badger itself. And I was astounded to see badgers mentioned in the same breath as Siberian tigers in *The Great Soul of Siberia*, by Sooyong Park (Collins, 2016), when he was writing about early lessons adult tigers teach their cubs, lessons that included "… badgers are tasty but have a temper and a long, sickle-like nail that can really cut you …" Thus, the badger's reputation for fearlessness in a tight corner is ennobled in my eyes.

Mind you, the weasel's reputation is also built around punching above its weight. The late David Stephen, a Scottish naturalist and writer of distinction and a bit of a specialist on the weasel tribe, wrote of it thus in *The World Outside* (Gordon Wright, 1983): "... a mighty atom – a mink in miniature, a 2–4oz mustelid delivering a thousand volts, a fire-cracker in brown topcoat and white waistcoat who can put the fear of death in many a grown man."

John Buchan, who knew his way round the flora and fauna of the land, reached for the mighty atom to portray the mindset of Fish Benjie in his immortal *John Macnab* (Nelson, 1925): "Benjie fought in no orthodox way, but like a weasel, using every weapon of tooth and claw, but in his sobbing furies he was unconquerable, and was soon left in peace."

I stayed still, leaning against the tree. In five minutes the weasel reappeared, lingered in the entrance for about ten seconds then advanced into the sunlight, followed at once by a single-file platoon of eight more weasels, which was presumably the whole family. They flowed along the lane in goose formation, a rippling ground-level skein of tawny and white, a breaking wave of terror in the collective awareness of the mice and vole population of that place and everything else up to and including the rabbits, maybe even the hares. And clearly they have no fear of badgers.

So there is a scruffy little country lane I know, and it has a dark wood with a badger sett, and from time to time the tenants from hell move in.

*

There is a vast old beech tree, a felled giant, lying prone across the top corner of a hillside clearing where Stirlingshire begins to climb from the Carse of the Upper Forth into the first and last of all the mountains of the Highlands – the first if you are travelling north out of Stirling, the last if you are travelling south towards it. The sett is an old one, the farmer whose land it dignifies told me once it was easily a hundred years old – "my family has been talking about them since forever". He thought the beech was slain in the 1960s in a winter of huge winds. It's a landmark in their everyday world, a constant presence mouldering away at the speed of the wildwood, which is very, very slow. The combination of its vast root plate and its sprawl of mighty limbs contrived to hold the trunk clear of the ground along much of its length, and the grooved path that flows beneath it linking the sett to the woods is of the badgers' making. In the earliest months of my badger watching, it became a landmark in my everyday world too. A step up among the disintegrating limbs and a precarious balancing act back towards the roots hoisted me to a perch seven or eight feet above the ground, a priceless vantage point beyond which the sett and its clearing sprawled away south and east and downhill, a no-man's land neither Highland nor Lowland, but well on the way to both. But because it wasn't enclosed like a hide, I had 360 degrees of visibility and a wide wedge of sky at my disposal.

In many ways it symbolised why the Highland Edge terrain has proved so invaluable to my nature-writing life, for it teems with the wildlife tribes of both Highlands and Lowlands. On any dusk or dawn, and depending on the season, I might see roe and red deer, red squirrel, hen harrier, three kinds of owl, three kinds of geese, mute and whooper swans, curlew, buzzard, fox, pine marten, otter, peregrine, among much else, and (if its hunting mission had been a successful) a rainbow trout hurtling through the treetops slung from the undercarriage of a homing osprey. And badgers.

For months after I had discovered the couped-over beech, I was so preoccupied with the wider landscape, the badgers and their neighbours and fellow travellers, that I had paid no attention at all to the tree itself. One evening, I had come down from the highest part of the trunk and spent the last hour of my watch leaning against the lowest part for a different perspective, a rearrangement of the landscape down to badger level. The trunk had no bark left on it. Time had smoothed its surface to pale grey skin. That evening, I looked at it closely for the first time, and what caught my eye was a pattern of marks in parallel lines grouped in threes and fours and which began and ended abruptly. They cut across the grain of the wood, so they were not *of* the tree. They were badger scratch marks. I had spent my hour by the badgers' scratching post without realising it. Until that moment, the scratching posts I had seen were on standing tree trunks. But these were on a horizontal trunk and more or less at ground level. So, what were they for? I decided to consult Ernest Neal. In *The Natural History of Badgers*, he wrote: "When a badger uses such a tree, it gets up on its hind legs, reaches as high as it can with its front paws and then brings them down, scraping them against the bark as it does so ... This action has been described as claw sharpening, but that is clearly incorrect, as no such action will sharpen the claws, rather the contrary ..."

He suggested three explanations. One – that it tones up muscles after sleeping, the way many an animal stretches when it wakes. Two – that it helps to free mud from between the toes after foraging, citing the presence of mud on many a scratched tree. But that's for trees with bark. I liked Ernest Neal's third try best, especially the last sentence:

> *Another possible explanation is that a scratching tree serves as a visual or scent signal which would have a territorial significance. It is known that*

the wolverine, which is a near relative, marks trees near its den, but this appears to be due to repeated chewing and biting. Consequently the trees become very conspicuous and may serve as visual signals. Unlike the wolverine, badgers are mainly nocturnal so a scratching tree is unlikely to act as a visual sign for them, but it may well act as a scent marker … You will also find scratch marks on fallen trees which indicate repeated rather than random use. It is clear that more observations are needed before the full significance of these "scratching" places is understood.

A wise and untypically open-minded badger guru was Dr Neal. And that was after fifty years of watching badgers. He reminded me of a conversation I once had with David Stephen when he was in his mid-seventies and not long before his death. I asked him if he still harboured ambitions in his dealings with wildlife after a lifetime devoted to its cause. "Just one," he said, "I want to know more about it."

Barn Owl

That modest elevation offered by the badger sett's couped-over beech taught me something about watching wildlife. All the badger activity was on the ground – obviously – but the airspace immediately above the clearing was suddenly no less intriguing. Not the airspace you looked up into where an osprey or a red kite or a roding woodcock might cross the clearing and leave the sense of itself on the air after it vanished, like a vapour trail; rather it was the airspace a yard or two or three above the ground, confined to the eye-level fliers whose sphere of interest lies mostly in depths of grass and bracken fronds and orchid leaves. Night after night in that wood I watched a masterclass in the silent art of low-level flight. Barn owls and I are familiars in each other's eyes. They introduced themselves to me when I was very young and, even now, every new encounter stirs in me the born-again sense of that small boy with the unruly fair hair and the freckles and the blue eyes.

Prefab childhood in 1950s Dundee was lived more outdoors than in. The prefabs were neatly buttoned to a west-facing hillside along the last street in town, and the farmland of Angus began across the road. Fields were as much for playing in as growing crops, and the neighbours I liked best were autumn and winter geese, spring and summer skylarks.

The entrance to the farmyard was no more than a quarter of a mile from our prefab, but it was forbidden territory. It was inhabited by what Grassic Gibbon would have called "coarse brutes". I hid when I saw them coming. But the stackyard was a different proposition from the farmyard. I thought of it as no-man's land. It belonged to the farm, of course, and farm things happened there, but it was a frontier land between farmyard and street, and its fence was flimsy. Mine was the kind of childhood that paid little heed to flimsy fences.

Haystacks were flimsy, unchancy creatures, especially at night. They seemed to stand around for weeks or months and grew dishevelled in gales and downpours. Voles, mice and rats and God knows what else sped along the curved alleyways between stacks, and barn owls loved voles, mice and rats as much as I loved barn owls. So my first barn owls coursed silently through my most impressionable years, low-flying, head-down hunters that tilted and swerved on one wingtip or the other as daylight faded over the Firth of Tay far below. The darker the night, the brighter the face, the breast and the underwings of the moping, mopping-up owl, and the more predatory its grip on my young imagination.

The farm was a run-down place with run-down barns, and these are the barn owl's favourite kind. Any evening I happened to be walking home that way, there was always the chance of meeting head-on and at close-quarters the fair, heart-shaped face of the haunter of no-man's land. These were encounters with nature at the edge of things, the edge of the town, the edge of the countryside, the edge of the day and night and the edge of my comfort zone, beyond which the black outline of the farm buildings bleakly inked in my discomfort. But the edge of things has since become my preferred terrain – the edge of the land, the edge of the sea, islands beyond the edge of the sea, the edge of the Highlands and the edge of the Lowlands wherever the two have been in constant collision for the 10,000 years that fashioned the known world, or, if you prefer, since the beginning of time.

Barn owls, then, are ambassadors for life on the edge.

Those childhood barn owls survive only as a patchwork of memories, glimpses as unrevealing as moths darting in from the darkness to dance at a flame and disappear again; impressions of a few seconds of flight at a time and on the far edge of the insipid glow of streetlights, always fading into that other world where owl and farmyard conspired to do whatever it was they did together. Except once.

That once was when I was lured by forces beyond my control across no-man's land and into hostile territory beyond the stackyard. It was the first time I saw a barn owl fly in daylight. It was a sunny early morning. The owl appeared among the stacks, its beak clamped on a mouse that hung down like a moustache (ah, a mouse-tache), and I had never seen *that* before either. It vanished round the corner of the nearest building, reappeared seconds later spotlit by the sun against the dark background of a second building. I had never so much as looked at that more distant building before but now I saw that its door leaned open at an odd angle, and that through the doorway I could see gaps in the slate roof.

The owl banked left and flew inside.

An owl that lived inside a building was not a possibility I had ever considered before. Moments later, it was out again, minus the mouse. I was still trying to come to terms with this discovery of a bird living inside a building when a second barn owl flew out through the broken-down door of the broken-down barn. My first thought was that it might be a brother of the first owl, because I had one and we were accustomed to going in and out of the same door at home.

Then an owl flew back in. The same owl? The first owl? A different owl altogether? How many owls were in there, and why was the building so important to them? My curiosity became an irresistible force, propelling me through the stackyard to the corner of the nearest building. For the first time in my life, no-man's land was behind me instead of a barrier in front. I flattened against the wall. I had seen cowboys do this in films. I peered round the corner. Coast clear. I inched sideways along the gable to the next corner. I was now deep in forbidden territory. Between me and the owl door was a wide open space deeply rutted with mud and liberally dowsed with cowshit, which I would have called country pancakes at the time. Almost certainly, I would have been wearing sandals, short socks and short trousers. I was not dressed for this.

If there had been people around, if there had been tractors, horses, herds of cows, or any one of the tribe of coarse brutes I loathed and feared, I would have left. But no one and nothing moved. Only the smell troubled me, but a bad smell was no more deterrent than a flimsy fence. I ran across the farmyard and straight in the door of the owl barn. Within, all was conspiratorially black. Then something muttered up near the roof. I looked up into a white, heart-shaped face and in that moment the barn owl claimed me as a friend for life.

It tilted its head at right angles, so that the heart-shape looked like a butterfly, then it straightened up again and was heart-shaped again. The owl stood on some kind of shelf where the wall met the roof. Right next to it was a pile of grey stuff that looked like a cross between wool and used Brillo pads. It would take years before I realised what it was made of ... regurgitated owl pellets.

A second owl drifted past me somewhere near the floor and rose without a sound to the same shelf and stood beside the first owl, then both birds did the sideways head trick. The second owl sat on the pile of grey stuff. Then a tractor engine fired up in the distance and my awareness of where I was and what I was doing and what would happen to me if I was caught rushed in the door like an icy wind. The owl-spell shattered and I had wings on my feet. I was over the flimsy fence and halfway home before I stopped running.

"I fell in the field," I told my mother as she first looked at me then caught the smell of cows. But something fundamental took root that day and I reap its harvest still. I had charged into no-man's land, crossed into enemy lines, lived to tell the tale and returned a warrior for nature's cause. Barn owls did that.

*

The farm is long gone, likewise its barn owls. Bungalows live there now. There is another mile or more of Dundee beyond what was the last street in town of my childhood. It would take another forty years or so before I found another barn owl haunt that captured my imagination with something like the same force. It lay at the end of a track on a quiet headland in the south of the Isle of Skye. It had in common with the farmhouse the inexorable ruination of an old stone building, and the opportunist presence of barn owls. Its name is Suisnish.

A single-storey cottage subsides slowly into a bare clifftop, wide open to ocean winds from the south-west. The view from its back "garden" (a piece of land now indistinguishable from the sheep-and-cattle-shorn terrain of the headland) gazes at the Skye Cuillin, at the mountainous, ocean-going profile of Rum, at sunsets painted on daydreams, and all of that was seared into the hearts and minds of hundreds of nineteenth-century islanders whose fate was determined by the architects of the Highland Clearances. Barn owls quested among the waist-high ruins of the abandoned township of Suisnish, whose very name is shorthand for one of the Clearances' bleakest episodes. Seabirds crammed the airspace and, in addition to the cruising golden eagles, sea eagles have returned to a land from which they were exterminated more than a hundred years ago. But not the people, not here.

The cottage at the end of the track is later than the cleared ruins. Its roof was more or less intact.

I had known the place for quite a few years before I looked in at one windowless window frame and a barn owl flew out of the doorless doorway. The moment induced a spasm of recognition that reverberated all the way back to my Dundee childhood.

Suisnish inhabits a landscape whose natural ecosystem was obliterated by overgrazing. The free-range presence of sheep, cattle and red deer tormented the ruins and defaced the melancholy inheritance. But the barn owls' breathless beauty there offered a scrap of life to mitigate the melancholy. Ours is the only species so hell-bent on taking nature on, hell-bent on taming it, obliterating it where it suits us. Yet whenever we turn our backs on some outrageous human endeavour, from Gruinard Bay to Chernobyl, nature begins to move in at once, lays ground cover, plants trees, soothes broken stones with moss, summons moths and dragonflies, swallows, orchids, wolves. Barn owls.

Suisnish offered rarefied barn owl watching. Be there at sunset and linger into the gloaming (and if you have the tolerance for it, on into moon-and-starlight). Sunset drapes itself over the two Cuillin ranges of both Skye and Rum, insinuates itself into all the intervening tracts and inlets of the Atlantic. Mountains smoulder with echoes of their volcanic infancy. The soundtrack is seabirds in passing and lingering hordes and wanderers – gannets, greater black-backs, fulmars, auks and Arctic terns overlaid with the soulful chants of eiders and grey seals. The whole can overwhelm watching eyes for want of a focal point. But while my back was turned on the cottage, the hunting barn owl slipped out through the black rectangle of the doorway, flew round two walls of the cottage (the shadowed front, the ocean-lit south gable), then burst with devastating slowness and silence into that fizzing airspace like a sudden waft of bog myrtle scent in a new rainfall. And then I had my focal point.

A barn owl is unarguably beautiful in any light, and for that matter in no light at all. But now it wore electric copper on its back and upper wings, the back of its neck and upper head; deep pink on its face, breast and underwings. And as it flew south to north and crossed the fieriest flare of the afterglow between me and the point where the sun finally sank behind Gars-bheinn, the whole bird was a shadow rimmed in burning gold. With binoculars raised, my response to such beauty approached the limits of self-control. In the background were the out-of-focus pinnacles of the Cuillin, a pageant of mountain superstars that blurred past until the owl ran out of mountains. At more or less the same moment, the owl wheeled south again, dipped towards the clifftop and began sifting among the ruins of the cleared township, unsettling mice and voles and the ghosts of the cleared people. Occasionally it stopped on the air, lowered long blond legs and feigned a stoop, or thudded softly into the grass or the nettles that thrive within forgetful, broken walls.

The barn owl's strike rate is not high. In perhaps twenty minutes during which it was hardly out of my sight, it stooped six times and made no kills. Then it vanished below the level of the clifftop and I wondered how close to the waves it might descend. Then I wondered why it was here. The Hebrides and the West Highland mainland are not barn owl strongholds. How did it end up here?

That moment of the owl's descent towards the waves recalled a kestrel I once watched in Orkney. I saw it several times over a week and it hunted constantly along the very edge of the tide, hovering out over the waves to make the most of an offshore wind. I never did see what it was trying to catch. I wondered if mice and especially voles rummage for food in seaweed. Orkney has its own sub-species of vole, after all, so it is reasonable to suppose that by Orkney's very nature, it will turn up along the shore. And if it happens there, why shouldn't it happen on Skye, along the coasts of narrow projections of land like Suisnish's headland?

After the owl's departure from the clifftop, I settled back for a while by an old stone wall no higher than my head when I sat against it. My view was raw and compelling and with a palpable suppressed power that was far beyond anything you might describe as simply beautiful, and that power only strengthened as daylight departed. The sky paled to almost white in the north-west, and everything that was bare rock in all its forms darkened to a profound blue-black and seemed to advance en masse to exaggerate purposefully its physical presence on every watching eye and listening ear, like a wolf pack when it howls.

My fondness for the gloaming is a companionable trait for watching owls, likewise my capacity for sitting still. It is time spent tuning in, becoming landscape. I reasoned the owl might be back. I watched the mountains. I waited. An hour drifted by and summoned the moon up out of the ocean. Ghostly analogies are everywhere in the literature of barn owls, and if that shows a lack of imagination among generations of scribes, it is an understandable lack. Mostly they wear ghostly shades, mostly they are seen in low light, mostly they move with what we think of as a ghost's gait. Without subscribing to the barn-owl-as-ghost analogy, let me say this: when the owl finally materialised not ten yards from me like a wad of blossom on a wind-crippled rowan tree, it drew a gasp from me, which by the time it had escaped into the air was most of the way to being a small shout of astonishment.

Clearly, owl and rowan were familiar collaborators, the chosen perch offering clear sightlines along several alleys between old stone walls, alleyways such as a mouse or a vole might use to navigate through the island night. But the barn owl can also turn its head through 180 degrees, so that it instantly homes in on the slightest sound behind its back. The owl surveyed its portion of the island from the rowan and only its head moved. When it flew at last, it travelled no further than the end of the rowan's moonshadow before it fell, feet first, and disappeared behind the far wall of the ruin where I sat. I saw nothing of what happened next until, with a wide banner of white wings and a scuffle of talons, it announced itself on the topmost stone of the ruin's broken gable. A vole hung from the beautiful heart-shaped face, held there by the odd curve of its broken back.

A handful of seconds later and it was gone. Just as suddenly, the darkness seemed to fall like a dropped shroud. Then the moon climbed above the Cuillin ridge, a heaven-scent moon for the hunting owl and for the owl watcher with roosting notions.

Skylark

The Architect of Song

Blue, sang a skylark,
and singing, drew
a blue column of song.

Song column! thought a hawk
and thinking, knew
there was a lark on top.

Red, drew a talon,
and drawing, slew
the architect of song.

Silence, found a skylark,
and finding, chose blue
and song

and began to draw
the column anew
on the field's red-smudged page.

West of the Daylight Moon

Just west of the daylight moon and hard on the heels
of the shroud of a departing thundercloud,
a skylark reintroduced the thunder-dumbstruck land
to singing.
Then lark after lark they rose and their songs
fell to earth as flakes of ringing silver
that cracked a smile on the stone-deaf frown
of Beethoven.
His inner ear stirred and his quill hand
crossed page after page, for the larks
had reintroduced him to singing
and symphony.
And the dumbness of deafness turned and fled
just as the thundercloud had roared then yielded
to the silent but more glorious furies of rainbow
and larksong.

Poetry is taking risks with language, but if it's nature poetry you have in mind, you must still adhere to nature's laws even while you explore literature's risks. It is its own art. And the chances are that no matter which of nature's tribes enthral you most, sooner or later you will try to write a poem about skylarks. Because, there is something in the untutored art of larksong that kindles in a human breast a species of benevolent envy. Which of us would not like to be able to step up from the earth without preamble and ascend vertically, improvising such music as we rise? There is nothing head-turning about the physical form of the skylark, but once it is up and rising and singing, it turns every head within earshot, every squinting pair of eyes. Where is it? We don't want to know because we love to look at it, we just want to see the singer sing. With skylarks, the song is everything.

One of the most likeable traits of high summer is warm winds; unhampered warm winds down from the mountains that command low, rounded summer-grassy hillsides to sway to their rhythms. On the north and north-west-facing slopes of the Ochil Hills above Sheriffmuir, a little to the north of Stirling, and on an afternoon of late June, such a wind was at work on such a hillside. The arc of mountains that gave the wind birth and sent it on its way sprawled in summer blue finery all along the horizon. The wind furrowed the broad brow of the Ochils as it cruised the tall grass and heather tussocks and clusters of bog cotton, creasing the hillside's open face with laughter lines, opening and closing sudden mouths in the grass with every gust. In such a wind, the ancient hillside stillness of this corner of the massif was youthfully animated and sunlit deep green.

And this was a skylark hillside caressed by a skylark wind. The particular demands of skylark flight were surely never so effortlessly simple as they were on such a day on such a hillside and in such a wind.

There, poised on a tussock, was a brown study of fish-scale patterns in orderly rows, the tail garnished with giveaway stripes of white edging, the top-knot crest up-curved to a smooth point. The bird awaited a signal from the wind, a thumbs-up, an urging gust. Lift-off was gentle, silent. Transformation from gentle incline and silence to vertical columnar flight and song took a handful of seconds, a few feet of ascent. The song was full-throated from the first note, as self-confident as the opening bars of Beethoven's "Fifth" or Armstrong's "West End Blues". No preamble, no hint of the glories to come. The glories started with the downbeat.

There is a swatting character about the wingbeats, for they are designed to produce vertical lift rather than forward momentum. It cannot be a technique unique to skylarks among all the birds of the air, but in the skylark it is uniquely deployed. On a hillside like this one where there are many skylark nests, there are also many low-level flights during which the fliers look much like many other small brown birds on the wing. But the skylark deliberately selects a strikingly different flight technique for the vertical climb, and for which sustained song is apparently essential. Either that or it is the other way round and the flight technique is essential to project the song. It is not designed to climb in easy spirals like a sparrowhawk, or to power-climb like a golden eagle, or to streak up in erratic diagonals like a swift with its mouth open, a turbo-charged fly-trap. Instead, the skylark climbs backwards, or at least back-first, and all the while shedding shards of song.

Larksong and larkflight are, of course, tools of biology and evolution, and have been for who knows how many millennia, but for a handful of centuries now they have also provided the raw material for poetry.

Norman MacCaig, for example, in "Landscape and I": "That sprinkling lark jerked upward in the blue."

"Sprinkling" is inspired. The lark climbing above me in the Ochils sprinkled the hillside with discarded notes. And yes, that arguably un-poetic "jerked" is spot-on too, a telling observation of the nature of the rising flight.

George Mackay Brown, for example, in "A Child's Calendar": "A lark splurges in Galilees of sky …"

Who but a poet with such an ear and such an eye for nature's particularly Orcadian tendencies would bracket "lark" and "splurges" side by side in the same line? But as I climbed the hillside, lark after lark rose ahead and behind and to left and right, such ostentation as a means of announcing territorial rights and ambition, is a living breathing definition of the verb "to splurge", yet it took a great poet to wed it to such circumstances.

And: "... what peltings of song!" He wrote that about skylarks, too, in "Following a Lark" for that drenching downpour of larksong en masse when "sprinkling" is just too genteel for what falls to earth.

And then, of course, there was this:

> Hail to thee blithe Spirit!
> Bird thou never wert,
> That from Heaven, or near it,
> Pourest thy full heart
> In profuse strains of unpremeditated art.

Percy Bysshe Shelley, the crown prince of skylark poets, certainly knew the value of an immortal opening verse with which to ensnare his readers. "To a Skylark" layers imagery as thickly as semi-quavers in a climbing yard of larksong. It is arguably churlish and a bit picky to challenge the poem's reputation with a sliver of doubt, even if I am pretty sure I spent longer accumulating that doubt than he did listening to his single skylark – if, indeed, a single skylark is what he heard. "Heard", please note, not "saw":

> In the broad daylight
> Thou art unseen, but yet I hear thy shrill delight ...

He cannot see his skylark! So how can he be sure that he is hearing only one? I have good eyesight and good binoculars, but in a single concentrated hour of watching – and listening – on that Ochils hillside I realised that often the song of one skylark was replaced or at least overlapped by the new song of another, closer to me or lower in the sky and therefore louder. Shelley gives no clue that the possibility has occurred to him. It is possible, of course, that there was only one skylark singing and that he heard the song from beginning to end, but he does not tell us that he listened to the whole song. The skylark is still singing when the poem ends with a plea that surely still resonates with any nature poets who were ever stopped in their tracks by a singing skylark:

> Teach me half the gladness
> That thy brain must know;
> Such harmonious madness
> From my lips would flow;
> The world should listen then – as I am listening now.

The last verse, immortal as the first, redeems the whole by alighting on the nature writer's condition. How do we penetrate the minds of nature's creatures? How do we see the world as they see it? Then how do we articulate the harmonious madness and write it down? Skylark or skunk, whitethroat or whale, wagtail or wolf, butterfly or bear – why do they do what they do, and how do they decide, and what do they think of us? The questions vex us as they vexed Michel de Montaigne in his *Essays* of 1693: "The defect that hinders communication betwixt them and us, why may it not be on our part as well as theirs? 'Tis yet to determine where the fault lies that we understand not one another, for we understand them no more than they do us; by the same reason they may think us beasts as we think them."

*

Meanwhile, the nature of one particular hillside on one particular day sloped away below the singers as soon as they took off, and because this particular wind washed down from the north-west and met this particular north-west-facing hillside head-on and curved uphill as it did so, generating thermals, and because the wind was warm ... then every skylark lifted from this of all hillsides, on this of all days, in this of all winds, with thistledown ease. And then I became aware of a change in the nature of the song, a change so conspicuous that I began to think that the purpose of the song had also changed. This was not a territorial proclamation for the benefit of other skylarks. Suddenly, it reached my ears in short snatches a few seconds at a time, and with (it seemed to me) a hint of urgency. Whenever it stopped, I heard other skylarks further off, much higher up, and singing as they climbed. Then the urgent song kicked in again and drowned them out. What was going on?

Anyone who has tried to pinpoint a climbing, singing skylark from the wavering nature of the sound knows the difficulty.

Where is it?

Higher? Much higher?

Lower? How much lower?

But I could not remember hearing this other larksong before, and I confess to being briefly baffled. Nothing new there – it happens all the time. Then all was revealed.

I had been looking much, much too high. Even a dozen feet off the ground was too high. Even eye-level was too high. The singer, now that I had found it, was standing on a tussock not ten yards away and it was very definitely watching me. No one ever wrote a poem about a skylark on the ground.

So now the new questions began.

How long has it been there?

How long has it been trying to attract my attention?

And why?

Every few seconds it would sing for a few seconds then stop and stare through the one black eye I could see, then it would sing again for a few seconds more. The little rhythmic ritual went on and on. In the short silences, all the other singing birds of the hillside drifted in and out of earshot so that I heard them adrift and unfocused. Then the song from the tussock snapped back in and re-established the focal point. Shelley never heard this. Or if he did, he didn't put it in his poem.

The bird was edgy. It took me longer than it should have to realise that the bird had a nest nearby and the place I had chosen to sit (thinking I was outside the periphery of the hillside's nesting territories) was too close to it for the bird's comfort. So it sang *at* me in a way that was different from all the hillside's other singers because its purpose was different: it wanted to attract my attention and hold it, and (perhaps – I was guessing) convey to its mate and every other skylark within earshot that I was in their midst and my presence was troublesome.

Then it dawned on me: this was a variation of the broken wing trick with which skylarks try and lure intruders (with and without wings, and with two legs or four) away from the nest. No sooner did the thought lodge than the skylark flew a few yards and perched on another tussock ever so slightly closer and began to repeat the whole process. I moved away conspicuously, so that it knew I was leaving. It flew a few more yards, perched on a third tussock, sang again. *Go away, good riddance*, it sang.

*

Skylarks are my good omen birds. Where there are skylarks, there is hope. A few years ago, I drove 250 miles to catch a ferry to South Ronaldsay on the Orkney side of the Pentland Firth, there to drop into a purpose-built visitor centre then walk a mile across the low green island sward to the low green curve on a low bright clifftop that marked the 5,000-year-old Stone Age wonder that is the Tomb of the Eagles. The walk was anthemed by allegro skylarks and adagio curlews, and every footfall was dusted by ground-hugging, wind-cheating flowers – eyebright, primrose, spring squill, marsh orchid, grass of Parnassus. I walked from one oystercatcher territory to another, so the decibels of strident variations on a theme of "piss off" rose and fell about my ears with the rhythm of waves on shingle. Lapwings lined up strafing runs out of the sun and aimed a few feet above my head. They also fell out repeatedly with the nearest oystercatchers. Once, an Arctic skua, a dark and beautifully lethal missile of a bird, sped above the fields trailing a wake of six lapwings. The sea shone, gannets fell and rose and dazzled, seals crooned. And above it all, skylark after skylark after skylark sang and sang and sang on honeyed winds. There was never a less appropriate preparation for crawling inside a tomb in which the skulls and bones of sea eagles had been interred with the skulls and bones of Stone Age islanders.

My purpose was research for a book called *The Eagle's Way* (Saraband, 2014), which explored changing relationships between sea eagles and golden eagles following sea eagle reintroduction into east coast landscapes, and between sea eagles and ourselves. There was also a deep personal connection that coloured my response to the Tomb of the Eagles, for which I refer you to *The Eagle's Way*. To enter the tomb was to abandon the skylark-scrolled, sun-smitten, ocean-scented island overworld for a deeply affecting glimpse of the Stone Age from the inside of its corpse. The tomb itself harboured an extraordinary atmosphere, part sacred, part grim, part architecturally astounding, all of it to accommodate a pact between humans and eagles, life and death shorn of all adornment. I imbibed as much of it as I could handle while the uniqueness of the moment seared itself deep inside me; and if I was convinced of the existence of a human soul, I might concede that it touched that inner depth. But I am agnostic at best on the matter of a human soul, and without its carrying capacity for dealing with the forces of those moments, it all became too intense and finally overpowering.

I fled for the bright end of the tomb's entrance tunnel. The rush of sunlight was like the embrace of helping hands.

From shoreline rocks I watched gannets and Arctic terns fishing and tried to order my thoughts, tried to rationalise a relationship between islander and eagle that had clearly been sacred, and how unimaginable was the embeddedness of the people in nature's scheme of things. Oh, what we must have known about living as nature then that we don't know now!

It was a long hour before I left that shore and retraced my steps back up towards the tomb. It looked demure, sun-drowsed, placid as a tidal pool at slack water. Now I could admire how the restoration project had honoured the original builders, how the tomb had been skillfully grassed over so that it fitted back into the fabric of the island, as it had once fitted into the fabric of the lives of the tomb builders.

And then, as sublime a gesture of healing as I have ever known, the kind of thing I am apt to refer to as the forgiveness of nature – a single skylark rose from the very crown of the tomb's grassy curve. Skylarks are my good omen birds. Where there are skylarks, there is hope. As long as there are skylarks, I can handle most things. And now a skylark sang at the Tomb of the Eagles.

The skylark that sang
at the Tomb of the Eagles

chiselled upwards a thin column
of runes, primitive truths

bound up in catchy slurs
and jazzy triplets, like Bechet

exploring the deep blues.
So it was when tomb-builders

made landfall at Isbister,
found biddable stone to chisel

runes and truths of their own
and set aside a portion of headland

and the next eight hundred years
to memorialise the passage of their days

across the face of the island
domed in an unlettered grave.

The eagle's anthem shaped
the struck harp of their song

and talon-and-bone they honoured them
as they honoured their own.

Aarkum the Bard squinted skywards
under his raised hand

towards the rising, improvising lark
and mouthed two prescient syllables:

"Besh – ay",
Song Island.

Skylark, eagle, builder, tomb –
it is all the same song.

It is all the same
unfinished song.

Sea Eagle

From the apex of its soaring, spiralling ascent on a spring morning of the most enticing thermals it had ever known in its young, wandering life, a four-year-old white-tailed eagle embraced all the world that is Assynt in a single sunrise-gold-eyed glance.

Let's guess – somewhere between 5,000 and 6,000 feet, one Canisp on top of another (for Canisp was the mountain directly beneath the level wingtip-to-wingtip stillness that pinned the eagle's taut circle to the flat roof of air where it paused) – the eagle was high enough to evaluate that land- and seascape's every possibility from its clutch of landmark mountains to its hundreds of watersheets, headlands, sea lochs and islands, its ocean.

That particular spring would mark the end of the eagle's wandering years. From a Hebridean sea cliff nest, it had already travelled as far north as Shetland, and had heeded some stray seduction of race memory to attempt the sea crossing to the coastal Norway of its Lofoten ancestors, but the north-east wind was so enthusiastically locked into a south-west-making furrow that the young bird yielded. It turned back and flew before the wind, then followed the south-making passage of humpback whales, because there seemed to be wisdom and purpose in it.

The eagle made landfall again in Caithness. From a high flank of Morven, it responded to the tug of an array of stand-alone mountains far in the west, each of them enthroned on space; it was a summons as inexplicable as any other in any other eagle's wandering apprenticeship. Now, with the spring opening up like the flower heads of purple saxifrage in a high corrie, the eagle paused, circling slowly and far above that summoning land, looked down on a long, slender loch shaped like an otter with its muzzle nudging the flat shore of Inchnadamph, its tail curving and tapering into Little Assynt.

And this eagle knew about otters. Its young, wandering years, dedicated to the diverse arts of feeding and surviving, had covered many hundreds of miles from the heart of the land to its furthest-flung extremities, and many of the landscapes would be spontaneously chosen, and somewhere along the line fate always takes a hand and moulds a particular bird to a particular land. Quite why one will choose a Cairngorms pinewood and one a sea cliff on Mingulay is part of the allure of the species for those of us who watch and wonder. Our eyes and our minds tell us that logic plays no part in it. Nature would tell us, if we cared to ask, that that is because we don't have eagle eyes and we don't think like eagles.

There is also this: we read too many field guides, and field guides deal in generalities, helping us to identify but not to understand. And in many of nature's tribes there is noticeable individuality for anyone with the inclination to notice. Just as a Scots pine sapling from Abernethy won't thrive if you transplant it to the banks of the Kirkaig, a sea eagle thirled to a heartland pine forest will exhibit different skills and traits from one that has learned its trade on the north-west coast and the Northern Isles.

And so a four-year-old sea eagle hanging on the air high above Canisp, finding sprawled far below its wide-open wings a loch that looked like an otter, might have registered the resemblance and taken it as a good omen. For this eagle knew otters.

The coastlines, river mouths and island shores of the eagle's young years were well populated with otters, and the ultimate generalist among predators (for such is the nature of sea eagles) had also become something of a specialist. It happens. The otters that haunt coastal waters like Assynt's endless succession of bays and sea lochs were always worth checking out, because they often haul ashore fish too large to be eaten in the water. Once otter and prey are on the land, they are on eagle terrain too, and the bird judges itself entitled to compete for the fish. No point in the otter dragging it back into the water, so either it must defend the fish where it stands, or more often than not, concede defeat. Especially if the eagle in question has evolved a particularly effective technique.

A few minutes of standing over a catch while the sea eagle closes in again and again with talons lowered and wings pounding is an ordeal most otters don't much care for. The sight of that seven- to eight-foot-wide wingspan closing in at eye-level is the most intimidating force in all nature that a West Highland otter must confront on land, and it calls for quick decision-making with potentially grim consequences for a wrong call. The otter stands with one foot on the midriff of the fish. The eagle rushes down, its shadow like a suffocating blanket for a moment; the otter ducks its head, then turns head and neck to watch along its back as the eagle tips a wing to execute a tight vertical turn and homes in again and again and again. As the presence of sea eagles consolidates in Scotland's north-west, and that particular confrontation becomes ever more familiar to otters (and to the otter watcher with the time and the patience to linger and watch and wonder), they are quick to learn when to try and stand their ground and when to concede, knowing that there are plenty of other fish in the North Atlantic shallows.

Among its many character notes, the sea eagle can be a singularly accomplished bully, a trait that wins it many meals consisting of creatures it did not kill.

So this young sea eagle still lingered where its climb had come to rest on its airy stance high above Canisp. That climb was deceptively achieved by way of the cloak of apparent ease with which it was disguised, and for as long as it lingered it was almost as if the eagle had nothing better to do; that series of tight and level circles on wide, unbending wings that appeared to anchor it to the apex of the climb ... that, too, had an aura of loitering without intent about it. But the purpose lay hidden beneath the cloak. For this was an eagle in search of a territory. Nature had whispered in the eagle's ear: "It's time." After the next annual moult, the white tail feathers would grow in, and these are the tribal crest of the mature bird, the white-tailed eagle. Its head and neck would pale, and that hooked slab of a beak would glow vivid yellow, a cross between a banana and a machete, the final flourish of a bird as head-turning and eye-catching as any creature in the roll call of all wild Scotland, just as Assynt is in the roll call of all Scotland's landscapes.

Alone in that sky, the young sea eagle broke its own spell with a suddenness that spoke of a creature newly aware of its own fully mature powers of flight. The wings folded, the bird fell.

It fell and fell, a bird in its own avalanche, a fragment of wildness let loose and folded into a streamline of exquisite purpose, spilling thousands of feet in seconds. The otter-shaped loch – Loch Assynt, of course – awaited its coming, a moment of destiny, a turning point, a moment of wild upheaval.

A hundred feet above the surface, the wings unfolded. The bird swooped up in a fast curve that took it clear across the water and into a low and level flight, into the orbit of Quinag, and this too had purpose. From that airy, land-scanning apex of the climb, the eagle had marked perhaps the whole of Assynt's least conspicuous feature, a blunt-topped rock that gathered up all the land to the west of the Bealach-Leireag, but the eagle had also recognised it as a landmark where eagles have landed forever. Creag na h-Iolaire, which in the language that named this landscape is Eagle Crag. There it landed on its own shadow, there it perched, there it grew still.

*

There are many such rocks across Highland Scotland that bear the same name. Some denote eagle nest sites, some are simply places where eagles like to perch and feed, some look like eagles when seen from the communities that named them. And here is the crucial factor for this particular white-tailed eagle: these rocks are known to be favoured by both Scotland's species of eagle, and also contested by them.

When a golden eagle appeared round a shoulder of Spidean Coinich, where it had been prospecting for ptarmigan, and pointedly changed course, it is safe to assume that the sea eagle on Creag na h-Iolaire knew what to expect. The golden eagle launched a shallow dive with wings half-folded. The sea eagle waited until the last moment and ducked. The golden eagle climbed, turned, dived again, and again, and again.

The sea eagle knew it wasn't in physical danger – this was gesture politics. It held still. When the fourth flypast dragged a talon along its lowered neck, it leaped in the air and with a kind of airy shuffle then landed again ten yards away. The golden eagle took possession of the rock. Honour, or something like it, was satisfied. Mostly, the two eagle tribes get on. Mostly, golden eagles nest higher than sea eagles. Mostly, sea eagles hunt the coasts. If it comes to a dispute in the air, the golden eagle almost always wins because, in every way, it is the superior flier. If it comes to a tussle on the ground over prey, the sea eagle can usually muscle the golden eagle away. They both know this. So, mostly, they get along.

Abruptly, the sea eagle flew, driven as much by hunger as anything else. It flew north-west, low above the bealach and through the glen beyond, down to sea level when it reached Loch Nedd, through the narrows before the world suddenly burst apart into the great maw of Eddrachillis Bay.

Almost at once there were eiders, a small raft of birds adrift among that shoreline scatter of tiny islands, skerries and anonymous rocks. At the first hint of the eagle's approach, they dived. The eagle circled, waiting. When they surfaced again, they were a tighter-knit group, a more difficult target. One drake swam alone, fifty yards away. The eagle made for it, knowing it would dive again. But the eider does not have eagle eyes and it does not think like an eagle. When it surfaced again, the eagle was there, poised in a singularly ungracious hovering manoeuvre. You might call it monstrous. The eider died somewhere in mid-air above the bay, held in the formidable grasp of the biggest, yellowest talons in all Scotland.

The burdened eagle swung in a low, wide circle above the ocean, and as it flew over the islands of Calbha Beag and Calbha Mor and faced south again, it tilted the whole mountain mass of Assynt with a simple adjustment of its wings and felt a sense of rightness regained, an awareness of an ancient bond between the tribe of white-tailed eagles and this place on its very own map of the world.

*

If the reintroduction of Scotland's sea eagles that began on Rum in 1975 could be said to be a second coming, then the east coast reintroduction that began in 2007 was a third. The reintroduction site was on Forestry Commission land in north-east Fife, the south shore of the Firth of Tay. That landscape is well populated by people and characteristically Lowland. The city of Dundee, of all places, is just across the river. Why "of all places"? Because the city of Dundee is where I began myself. So when I stand some midwinter dawn on a shore of the Tay estuary – any of its shores – and look around me, nothing and nowhere on earth is more familiar to me than this. This wider-than-a-mile moon river with my grey-brown home city heaped along its northern bank, those low, sheltering hills, that sluggish midwinter sunrise beginning to redden the North Sea horizon like a forge slowly warming to its task even as the moon dips behind upstream hills, the final daybreak flicker of a scatter of lighthouses all the way to the Bell Rock ... all that is the first of all my landscapes. It was where I tumbled into the world and fell more or less at once under nature's spell.

Dundee is a thousand years old and for all but the last two or three hundred years the natives would have known sea eagles. The last one in all Scotland had been killed in Shetland in 1920. For fifty-five years, they were gone from the land. For much of my life, the nearest eagles to the Tay were golden and aloof, and they haunted – as they still do – the high hills of the Angus glens thirty miles to the north of Dundee.

We are still getting used to this new definition of the word "eagle" in our hearts and minds, as well as our neighbourhoods, fields and woods and shores, and we will have to make our own accommodation with this extraordinary presence of nature, for nothing is surer than that the sea eagle is a bird that ruffles feathers.

Just how extraordinary a presence? Consider the impact on the eaglets' lives when they were still but a few weeks old: their capture in Norway, the alien and terrifying journey in an aircraft. Yet it seems they knew – precisely – their direction of travel and the course corrections along the way, *and remembered them*. For as long as people have been travelling from Scotland to the west coast of Norway to bring back sea eagle chicks in a sustained endeavour to reintroduce the species, some of those same birds, very occasionally and one at a time, have attempted to retrace in reverse the journey of the aircraft that brought them. One in particular made it back to Norway and stayed there to breed. Another Norwegian bird reintroduced into the west of Ireland was found exhausted on the sea cliffs of Aberdeenshire, and it would seem that it too was hell-bent on Norway. Others have cropped up in Orkney, and I have good cause to wonder what kind of race memory propelled them there.

There is also this. By the time this new phase of reintroductions began, there was already an established west coast population. The birds spread up and down the west coast from Torridon to the Mull of Kintyre, but established strongholds on Skye and Mull in particular. Mull is due west of the Firth of Tay. The first of the Fife birds to breed did not do so on the east coast, but on Mull. Like several other east coast birds, it had found its way right across Scotland, meeting and quite possibly being reassured by other eagles along the way, following the lie of the land and the course of the Tay, and who knows what other signals and traits of inherited memory. It settled among its own kind, and in a west coast island landscape very similar to the one from which it was removed in Norway. Others have travelled to Mull and back and may well have lured Mull birds with them, and that too is in the nature of this eagle some of us now find on the doorstep.

And what particularly commends those journeys to me is the astonishing coincidence that, for as long as I have been responsible for determining my own travels around my own country, I have sought out in particular and with ever increasing frequency the land between Dundee and Mull. The Tay becomes the sea just east of Dundee. It rises on Ben Lui, far to the west, and from the summit of which you can see at no great distance the hills of Mull. This, it seems to me now, is a destined connection. Wherever I have travelled in the decades since I moved away from Dundee and the shores of the Tay estuary, I have never quite succeeded in kicking the habit of leaving myself behind. I never stopped finding reasons to return.

I miss the huge skies of the east coast when I am gone, the salt air, the sea views unpunctuated by islands and the sunrises there. For if you are thirled by birthright to the east coast, your relationship with the sea is defined by the fact that the sun rises out of it so that it illuminates and galvanises the day ahead, whereas the west coast is a more melancholic beauty of lingering sunsets and earthly sorrows. I miss the city's old stones and the speech and hospitable good humour of the natives. But mostly I miss the glories of the river, and the bird hordes where it meets the sea, the winter rafts of thousands of eider ducks, the myriad wader tribes, the spring terns and the sea coast puffins, the kittiwakes eternally chanting their eerie non-de-plume a yard above the surf; the grey and the common seals lounging cheek by jowl on Tentsmuir's expansive sands, the bottlenose dolphins that have become increasingly familiar in recent years.

But never, never for a moment of wildest imaginings did I conceive the notion that my place on the map would spawn a new tribe of eagles, of all things. Yet here was where it began again, the third beginning.

*

Just as a Highland landscape can make a golden eagle look small at anything other than close quarters (and close quarters is not a situation golden eagles enter into often or lightly), so the gently rumpled and essentially Lowland landscape of the Firth of Tay can make a loitering sea eagle look like a Zeppelin. At first, the birds you were most likely to see here were young, and young sea eagles being sociable creatures, you could occasionally see Zeppelins in unlikely numbers. The RSPB's director of the east coast reintroduction project, Claire Smith, saw *eight* juvenile sea eagles soaring above her near the release site. I can only imagine what that looks like, but once, far from here, I watched from a clifftop *one* young sea eagle take off from a beach (thereby removing from the beach what I had dismissed from my lofty perch as one more grey rock among many), swing out over the sea in a wide, climbing arc so that it drifted towards my clifftop into the wind and, about fifty feet above my head, it held up against the wind and almost stopped, looking down. The bird was a dark grey silhouette against a dark grey sky on a dark grey and sodden day, but it still seemed as if it contrived to throw a shadow over me. The notional shadow of eight such birds in soaring close formation is perhaps the source of the primitive respect that impelled the tomb builders of Isbister 5,000 years ago.

The reintroduction programme is over now and there is a breeding pair in north Fife, another thirty miles north in the Angus glens. The release site had been a secret one, of course, although it was known to be on Forestry Commission land in north Fife, which narrowed down the possibilities, and this had been the landscape of countless bike rides in my younger years, and many subsequent and irregular visits on foot and on two wheels and four, so I knew my way around. I went quietly and alone in search of sea eagles.

There was a quiet hill road late one afternoon. The landscape it traversed had looked promising from the first, but I had seen no eagles on a number of previous visits. This time, I saw a small space where I could run my car off the road beside a field wall. Beyond the wall there was a long, narrow belt of trees, well-spaced and smallish oak, ash, rowan and holly. Beyond the trees a fence marked the edge of a field of rough pasture that dived steeply away downhill towards a snugly settled house with small outbuildings. Beyond the far edge of the field was a wood of bigger trees, a mix of conifers and bulky big hardwoods, and beyond that a steep hill face with scattered Scots pines high on one flank, bare on the other. All this enclosed a small glen, as if a misplaced portion of the Highlands had wandered off when the land was settling down from the ice age and, having ended here, it had shrunk to fit in with the rest of the landscape.

I found a tree to sit against, and which offered an unobscured view of the lie of the land. If it was a landscape on an intimate scale and fashioned into a human design, it had been adorned by nature. The effect had a harmonised quality that was easy to admire.

The young sea eagle is a vagabond. But having established base camp, it often wanders along beaten paths. When the Fife birds are in wandering mode, they mostly travel west along that notional eagle highway that ends on Mull (and often back east again); or else they go north and south up and down the east coast, doubtless puzzled by the sun that rises out of the sea instead of setting there. The ancient and – crucially – unbroken Norwegian sea eagle lineage into which the reintroduced birds were born, has no east coast to speak of, and it is possible that their instinct for many generations to come will be to seek out a sunset coast rather than a sunrise one. I think that, mostly, they will go west and settle there. But some have found the east coast to their liking and lingered. Before they fashioned nesting territories here, they acquired a home range here; not a territory – for it takes around five years for a sea eagle to reach breeding age, when territory takes on a completely different meaning – but a reference point and a place on their idea of the map of the world; a wooded hillside in north Fife not far from here, a place where they will quickly learn to exploit its every productive loch and hillside and goose-field, and the fish-and-bird riches of the Tay itself. In that context, a bare, sun-facing hillside, which was alive with rabbits, was also a perfect lure for the eagle watcher. It was surely only a matter of time, and I had plenty of that ...

*

Almost dusk. I just knew that all over the north of Fife and the south of Angus and up and down the entire length of the estuary from Tentsmuir Point to Newburgh, people had been having unplanned encounters with sea eagles, while I, having carefully staked out my territory and satisfied myself that I had identified prime sea eagle hunting and roosting habitat, had chalked up a squad of wood pigeons, a skein of overhead pinkfooted geese and an inquisitive robin. A buzzard had loped across the rabbit hillside, which emptied of rabbits in an instant. Now, in the glasses I could make out – just – that the distant hillside was aswarm with rabbits. The pines on their hilltop looked more inviting than ever, as if they had been added to the landscape just to accommodate roosting eagles.

At this point, the balance began to tip in my favour. I have long since learned to love the twilit hours. It is the time of day when almost anything can happen, when the dayshift begins to shut down, and owls to mobilise. While I waited, the moon rose and stood above the hill and conferred magic on the hour and the land.

Then they came in, directly above the Scots pines, and there were three of them at slightly different heights, working their wings slowly, wings like half-open parachutes, wings held briefly in stupendous down-curves, wings held straight and wide and tipped with primary feathers the size of paddles. With sea eagles, size *is* everything.

There was a wedge of clear sky between the pine-fringed slope of the hill and the inky profile of a nearer plantation forest. I had been studying that wedge of sky for hours, pleading with its very emptiness – and, in a moment, there were three eagles flying there, and the wedge of sky was suddenly devoid of space. The impact of these birds on the sight is astounding, but in the oceanic, mountainous west, the landscape feels as if it was born to accommodate such creatures, but in this little garden valley they seem to joust with the very hills for elbow room. They came round the hill like a slow arrowhead, the middle one of the three slightly ahead of the other two, one above and one below. I wondered if they had any idea at all of the collective impact they made on the lesser creatures of the world, not to mention the watching mortal in the edge of the wood. There was next to no light left, the sky behind them was pale grey, darkening towards the hill edge, and they were as two-dimensional charcoal birds newly drawn on that blank sheet of graduated greys.

Nothing else moved. Even the eagles seemed neither to advance nor retreat, rise or fall, as if they were content with their new portion of the sky and might roost there on the wing. The greying earth inhaled and held its breath, and in its silence three eagles had paused in the sky next to the evening hilltop I had thought might accommodate an eagle roost. Then they drifted south across the face of the hill, where they simply dematerialised against the fading light and the greying coalition of shadows.

Where did they go? Did they settle in the valley? There was a small wood of hefty trees down there near where there must be a rabbit warren. Or did they circle the hill and drift up to its summit trees from below and behind? Did they settle there among the east-facing branches, so that they could benefit from the first rays of the earliest light? There was a small loch to the east well stocked with fish and the haunt of wild duck, geese and swans, and none of these are safe from the sheer, weighted power of a hunting sea eagle.

I sat on for a darkening hour, wedged in against the woodland edge. The moon began to brighten the land despite its attendant cluster of clouds. It made the barn owl an easy spot, a shapeless patch of pale white adrift on the field edge far below, but moving with that easy lope that characterises its hunting gait. It was a heaven-sent moon for a hunting owl.

Curlews and oystercatchers began to drift inland, stabbing the quiet with their cries. A fox barked once. Pause. Again. Pause. Again, but was that third bark a different voice from within the wood at my back? If I was sitting on a straight line between two foxes, one of them might find me. Tawny owls laid round *ooh* vowels on the air, breathily soothing away the barked harshness.

And somewhere out there, up there, down there, or over there, three Norwegian-born sea eagles had settled into the deep shadows of a huge Victorian fir, or in the sparser shadows of the hilltop pines, or on a windless quarry ledge, or …

It was a strange, slightly eerie feeling to consider the new possibilities of that scattered flock of Scandinavians, forcibly re-nationalised as Scots, each of them making its own accommodation with its new life in this new land in various and unpredictable ways. Walking back to the car in the moon-tinted darkness, I felt energised by the awareness of what had just begun to unfold here, of a wholly unpredictable journey for all nature, and I decided that I would be a part of it.

*

A few days later, I slipped the car into the same roadside stance, silenced the engine and doused the headlights, and let the last hour of the early morning half-dark rush into the open window. I sat still while the warm engine muttered to itself the way warm engines do when they start to cool. I wanted to nullify the intrusion of my arrival before I headed out for the same tree at the top of the field. I like to be at peace with nature when I go to work. Almost at once I heard small soft wings. A wren. It was on a holly branch two yards away and at eye level. A wren at eye level is disconcerting. The eye is perfectly round and perfectly black and perfectly tiny. And there is only one eye because it looks at you side-on, so you find yourself wondering if the eye you can't see is watching something else.

The irony was potent. I was looking for eagles. I found a wren. In this landscape, the wren is the eagle's fellow traveller. We watched each other for perhaps a minute, which is a long stillness for a wakeful wren (though perhaps not for one that has just been rudely aroused from a pre-dawn doze). What disturbed our trance-like moment was the blackbird's arrival at the other end of the wren's branch. The wren dived down into deeper cover and was gone, the blackbird protested at something beyond my reach and vanished in the opposite direction. The holly branch was quivering and bare.

Fifteen minutes later I was back at the top of the field where I settled once more, this time to watch the valley empty of darkness and fill with light, eager for the next chapter of the eagles' story. The sky seeped colour into that very wedge between forest and pine-treed hilltop where the three eagles had materialised those few evenings ago. It was more or less due east of where I sat, and it began to fill hopefully with pale yellow and from the bottom up, so that it widened as it rose, a stain that spread south across the hilltop and between the pine trunks and tiny spaces between branches, then beyond the trees and down the far side of the rabbits' side of the hill. There it lingered long enough for me to register the presence of a small horde of rabbits all across the lower slope. Perhaps the eagles would home in there as soon as the light brightened. But instead it dulled to a wash of light grey travelling at twice its speed, a shroud of high cloud that precluded the spectacle of sunrise so that dawn stole furtively round the edges of the hill, disconsolation around the edges of my expectant mood. At this early stage of my slowly accumulating experience of watching sea eagles, I had seen three roosts – one above Loch Tay and two on Mull – and they were all on trees with an open outlook. And here were trees, not just with an open outlook but also rabbits for breakfast, not to mention that glimpse of three eagles one evening earlier in the week. I talked myself back from disconsolation to justifiable optimism.

When I finally saw a daylight eagle, its appearance first manifested itself as a disturbance of air, low and to my right and too far behind me for any kind of physical recognition to have been possible. There was a bellowing crow almost in my ear, then a second crow not far above my head, and both were furiously on the move. I twisted awkwardly round my right shoulder to see a sea eagle twenty yards downhill, ten yards inside the field, two yards off the ground, and swatting the air with gulping wingbeats the size of fireside rugs. The tail was startlingly white in so many shadows. The crows homed in on that tail from either flank, as if it was a target being towed along by the eagle for the purpose.

There was a moment of connection. The eagle, besieged by his black tormentors, suddenly looked upwards and left, and made eye contact. I now have a single defining image of that sea eagle pinned to the inside wall of my skull for my brain to look at whenever it needs one. The eye was pale yellow, darkly hooded and high in the profile of the head, which was lightly mottled pale grey and fawn, and just astern of that oversized, yellow, hooked slab of a beak. At the bottom of the wings' downstroke, and at such at close quarters and from slightly above, the bird revealed a corrugated drapery of up-curved feathers, folds and folds of feathers of such a size that they redefined the very word "feather". No part of what I could see looked like a bird shape; rather, there was a bluntly cornered and tilted triangle with the wing elbow at the apex, the tail feathers at the right corner and the primaries of one wingtip at the other. Only that eye, forehead and beak protruded beyond the smother of feathers.

The upswing began, the head vanished, the triangle collapsed and the moment was done. In its place there was an articulate eagle, low and unhurried over the field with two crows in thankless pursuit. The eagle contrived a mid-air convulsion that flipped the whole, improbably nimble mass on its back so that, instantly, the crows were confronted not with a white tail to torment but with a raised pair of fearsomely proportioned talons. It was enough. They wheeled away and vanished in the trees. The eagle reversed the manoeuvre and resumed its low-level flight, which appeared to have rabbit as its destination.

Such is the joyous unpredictability of being in the right place at the right time when something new turns up in a familiar landscape. Eagle and eagle watcher were making it up as we went along, and then revising what we made up. I had made my best guesses based on my frail grasp of sea eagle logic, not quite knowing whether such a thing even exists. I had settled on a particular corner of a particular landscape based on the little I thought I knew, only to have a sea eagle ambush me from behind. I watched it fly towards the rabbit field, but about 200 yards short of the field it banked and climbed and perched high in the open edge of that small plantation of big conifers. Then it began to preen, with a settled-looking I-may-be-some-time air. I scouted with the glasses all over the sky and in every corner of the land that was available to me from where I sat, but the preener in the tree was the only eagle in sight. So I decided while I waited for events to unfurl that I would try and reconstruct the sequence of events that had just unfurled behind my back.

Two possibilities occurred to me. One was that the eagle had flown up the edge of the field and I had not seen it simply because I was facing the other way. But the crows had only given voice at the very last minute when the eagle was already very close, and I know from many years of watching golden eagles that crows are smart, sharp-eyed, noticing creatures that will travel hundreds of yards to harass them, hurling abuse the whole way. It was clear that, here, the crows had travelled no distance at all to greet the sea eagle, and that could only mean that it had astonished them as it astonished me.

So the second possibility was this: the eagle was there all the time.

It was there, perched in the trees between the road and the field. Perched in the trees when its head swung round to glare at the nature of the intrusion represented by my car engine and headlights, relaxing again in the silence that followed when the sound and the lights died. Perched in the trees when the car door closed, not loud, but conspicuous at that moment in that landscape, the sound placed by the eagle precisely where the car engine had stopped. Perched in the trees and glaring at the place where I stepped beyond the fence into the field edge and began walking uphill towards its very tree, adjusting its head position minutely and moment by moment as I came closer. Perched in the trees when I walked *beneath* the very tree, not looking up but looking out across the field to the silhouetted hill with its pines, believing *those* trees might harbour eagles.

Still perched in the trees when I reached the high corner of the field and turned right, hugging the fence, taking pains to stay with the shadows so that I would not reveal myself to eagle eyes that might be scanning the dawn field.

By now the eagle's head had swung through 180 degrees, and it was still perched in the trees when I sat and grew still, and it decided I posed no threat, and that at least until full daylight came, stillness would serve its cause best. When daylight did finally arrive, the crows spotted the eagle and urged it on its way, but not perhaps until it flew, and it had fooled them all that time with its tree-coloured stillness. If it seemed to me to be extraordinary behaviour for an eagle, it was only because the eagle with which I was familiar was not this one, because a golden eagle would not be seen dead in Fife.

*

The east coast reintroduction has galvanised the presence of sea eagles in Scotland. They nest again on Hoy in Orkney, in the Angus Glens to the north of the Tay and at Tentsmuir in north Fife. I have seen them or heard of them on the Isle of May five miles off the Fife coast, in Berwickshire and in Galloway, in the Ochils near Stirling, in Highland Stirlingshire and Highland Perthshire, in the Cairngorms, in Argyll, and all across the north of the country and on many of the Hebridean islands. There is some evidence that young sea eagles and young golden eagles share roosts on their far-flung travels before they settle on a territory. It is a question of time, perhaps twenty years, perhaps less, before the sea eagle outnumbers the golden eagle. When that happens, it will restore the historical norm, and thanks to the far-sightedness of a handful of people who understand and admire eagles, nature will have taken back that which is rightfully hers and restored a crucial element of her colossal vision of the way things should be. And, by that time, our job will simply have become to stand back, watch and learn.

The Bit at the End

So, what is the best way to watch wildlife? Guess what: I don't know. I know what works for me at least some of the time, but I concede that I am a relatively rare species of wildlife watcher.

Firstly, I am not a naturalist and have never claimed to be one. Nor am I an ornithologist, and I am definitely not a biologist. I am one of the least scientifically inclined people I have ever met. I don't keep records of what I see and when and where.

What I am is a writer. I watch wildlife because it's what I like to write about, and in the process I hope I can assist nature's cause. In my heart of hearts I nurture the ambition that, from time to time, what emerges is literature. Anything that I may have to say about watching wildlife is in that context: I watch wildlife to write it down.

But for what it is worth, and in keeping with the character of this series of "In the Moment" books, the following may be useful. It is not a blueprint, not an instruction manual, but rather a series of suggestions, at best. If that sounds like a disclaimer in advance, that could be simply because I don't know anyone else who works quite like I do. Most of this advice has already appeared in the pages of this and many of my other books, either in implied or explicit form. What it amounts to is a way of working that has helped me over the years; some of it might just help you.

Choose your landscape

So, start with a landscape. Everything I have written that I judge to be worth anything at all has started with a landscape. It is the foundation of everything. What do you like in a landscape? Coast? Mountains? Trees? Rivers and lochs? Wetland? Low hills? Fields or croft land? I know, it sounds obvious, but thoughtful preparation about where to go will greatly improve your chances of seeing the kind of wildlife species that interest you.

Keep your distance

Avoid the beaten path. Get comfortable with being off-piste.

Blend in

Minimise your presence. Clothes matter. Blend in. Wear what's comfortable. You might be sitting still for a long time.

Sit tight

Speaking of sitting, have you got a good folding mat? And a bivvy bag underneath the mat gives you extra insulation (both are dirt cheap). If your chosen landscape happens to be Scottish, you will need them. Keeping your sitting parts dry and comfortable-ish could be a determining factor in whether or not you want to do this again.

Lean in

Find something to lean against. Trees work for me.

Stay quiet

Be still and be quiet. For best results, watching wildlife is a solitary pursuit. If you hate being alone and plan to watch in company, choose your company as carefully as you choose your landscape. Think kindred spirits.

Become part of the landscape

The purpose of all of the above is so that you can effectively become part of the landscape yourself. If your presence is so discreet and unobtrusive that wildlife will come towards you, that is when nature begins to share secrets with you.

Invest in good binoculars

Buy the best binoculars you can afford. If you don't use binoculars regularly, talk to someone who does. My current pair came from the RSPB shop at their Vane Farm reserve at Loch Leven. In a situation like that, you can try several pairs and get good advice.

Watch the middle distance

Now, with a good place to sit, a good mat underneath you, comfortable clothes that blend in with your surroundings and a decent pair of binoculars, learn to watch the middle distance. Even when there is nothing obvious to watch, constantly scan the land, the sky, the water and, especially, the middle distance.

Get lucky

Be lucky! I know there is nothing you can do about that, except that the more often you go out, the more often you watch, the more thoughtful your watching becomes, the luckier you get.

Repeat

Go again. Especially after the fruitless days (of which there will be many), be prepared to go back, to sit again.

Make notes

Take a notebook and something to write with.

*

The best advice I have ever encountered was in an exquisite little book unexquisitely titled *Autobiography* (it isn't an autobiography, it's a gem of close-quarters nature writing). It is by a writer called Margiad Evans and set in the English-Welsh border country, first published in 1943, and I quote it gratefully whenever I have the opportunity. She wrote this:

> *If you want to write with absolute truth and with the ease of a natural function, write from your eyes and your ears, and your touch, in the very now where you find yourself alive wherever it may be. Carry your paper and book with you and conceal yourself in the fields. Watch and be in what you see or in what you feel in the brain. There is no substitute even in divine imagination for the touch of the moment, the touch of the daylight on the dream.*

For my money, *that* is the best way to watch wildlife.

Jim Crumley is a nature writer, journalist, poet, and passionate advocate for our wildlife and wild places. He is the author of more than forty books, and is a newspaper and magazine columnist and an occasional broadcaster on both BBC radio and television.

He has written in depth on topics as diverse as beavers, eagles, wolves, whales, swans, mountains, native woodlands and species reintroductions, as well as being the author of a quartet of books on our changing seasons in the era of climate chaos, and the culminating work of his seasons project: *Seasons of Storm and Wonder* (2022). He lives in central Scotland.

Thanks to the editor, Craig Hillsley, and the proof-reader, Sahana Sambandam.

Also in the IN THE MOMENT collection

Writing Landscape: In this varied collection of essays, Linda Cracknell explores her inspirations, in nature and from other artists and their work, shows how her writing flows from her engagement with place, and offers prompts for the reader.

Philosopher–climber Francis Sanzaro shows that climbing is a sport of perception, a matter of mind as much as body, and in *The Zen of Climbing* he offers pathways into attaining the mindset required for effective, alert, successful practice.

Interpreting Dreams is both an invitation to pay more attention to our dreams and a toolkit for unlocking their hidden meanings. By bringing our awareness to the time we spend dreaming, we can become more present and fulfilled in daily life.

Permaculture: Planting the Seeds of Radical Regeneration. Practitioner and poet Maya Blackwell writes with expertise and personal experience of the transformative power of permaculture for both people and the planet. An essential resource in tackling the climate crisis.

Poet and essayist Kenneth Steven takes us on a series of meditative quests in search of his "atoms of delight"—treasures, both natural and spiritual—through some of Scotland's most beautiful landscapes. An evocative book that will inspire you to explore mindfully.

Acclaimed poet, memoirist and scholar Polly Atkin invites you to join her as she swims throughout the year in the lakes and rivers near her home in beautiful surroundings. You will be immersed in her quest for natural wellness and strength in a place of magical scenery. (FORTHCOMING)

Nature writer Anna Levin craves dark skies: the timeless joy of gazing upon stars and constellations; the stunning Northern Lights. She opens her ears to the sounds of owls and bats; feels the magic of song and story around a campfire. The night sky needs our protection. (FORTHCOMING)